BECAUSE IT'S TRUE.

FROM CONFUSION TO COMMUNION:
AN HONEST SEARCH FOR THE CHURCH
FOUNDED BY JESUS CHRIST

KRISTIE LILLEY

Paperback ISBN: 978-1-950043-62-0

Contents

Thank you, Jesus.

Preface

Dear reader,

This book is the fruit of a long and winding road—one marked by childhood trauma, deep unanswered questions, and years of spiritual searching. I'll save the full story for my memoir, but here's the snapshot: I spent years bouncing between various Christian traditions, always looking for solid ground. But my wounds eventually hardened into bitterness, and I started blaming God for my pain. That resentment led me away from Christianity altogether and into the occult, where I remained for over a decade.

But God, in His mercy, removed the scales from my eyes. When I finally returned to faith, I prayed earnestly that He would lead me to the truth—and to a true church. **I wasn't looking for a place that catered to my preferences, where the music was cool and the dress code was casual.** I wanted to go where **He** wanted me—whether I understood it or not, whether I liked it or not. I had followed my own intuitions before and saw where that lead me. And I had already exhausted the breadth of modern Christianity before. So after a year of deeply studying early Christian history, I began attending a liturgical tradition rooted in ancient practice. That path—though winding—led me back to something far older, far richer, and far more unified than I had ever encountered.

So how do we know if we're truly following **the real Jesus**, and not a version manipulated and shaped by modern culture, emotion, or false teaching? That question matters more than any other. Throughout history, people have used the name of Jesus to justify all kinds of con- tradictory beliefs. He Himself warned that many would come claiming

1

to represent Him, and that even the sincere could be led astray. It's not enough to simply say we know Him—we must be sure we're following **what He taught** and the path He laid down. This book is an invitation to explore that path more deeply. If truth matters—and it does—then knowing the real Jesus matters most of all.

That's why I wrote this book.

This collection of evidence is not an academic tome or an exhaustive apologetic work. It's a **personal and theological springboard**—a starting point to explore **how Christianity was lived, believed, and practiced from the very beginning**. It's the resource I wish I'd had when I started asking, *"What did the earliest Christians believe? How do I know if I'm in the right church? Who can I trust to know these answers?"*

It's designed for seekers, skeptics, and even lifelong Christians who may feel something is missing. My hope is to offer a foundation rooted in **Scripture, history, and the consistent witness of the earliest Christians**—those trained directly by the apostles themselves. A place where head and heart can finally meet in clarity. Afterall, faith and reason are not opposing constructs.

To help you go deeper, I've included:

- Scripture passages throughout *(All Scripture references are taken from the Holy Bible. Unless otherwise noted, quotations are from the RSV-CE.)*

- Citations from the Church Fathers, Church documents, and trusted scholars

- A carefully curated recommended reading list

- A citations and sources page for further research

If something here challenges you, good—lean into it. **Ask questions**. But be willing to be proven wrong. Seek the truth with a sincere heart.

I truly believe that if you do, God will reveal to you not just a church, but the fullness of the Christian faith that is ancient, enduring, and alive. Not a man-made ideology, not a modern reinvention, but the faith handed down from the very beginning—intact, sacramental, and still changing lives.

This isn't the end of the conversation—it's just the beginning. There are many top-notch scholars and apologists out there to help answer deeper questions, should they arise. What's most important is that **you pursue the truth at all costs.**

In truth and charity,

Kristie Lilley

The Long Way Home

I didn't grow up with catechism, creeds, or councils. Born an "Okie," I was raised in what I call "Standard American Christianity"—a mix of heartfelt sermons, altar calls, and emotional highs, played out in everything from living rooms to church buildings that looked suspiciously like shuttered Pizza Huts. There was no theological formation, no sacramental life, and certainly no continuity. Church attendance came and went, depending on what season of crisis I was in. Sometimes I'd go months, even years, without ever stepping foot inside a church. At home, trauma was a constant companion—divorce, abuse, and **instability colored my childhood and shaped the way I viewed God, love, authority, and myself.**

At sixteen, I was pregnant, married to an abuser, and quickly swept into the world of his parents' Assembly of God Pentecostal church. That is where I read the Bible from cover to cover and kept a *Strong's Concordance* nearby like a theological lifeline. I sang on stage. I was involved in the women's ministry. I prayed with boldness, hoping faith could fix what was broken inside me. I learned many valuable lessons during that time of my life and for that I'm thankful. But that is also where I learned the name-it-and-claim-it gospel, the kind that treats God like a vending machine and suffering like a sign of personal failure. **But while the language of victory echoed in the pews, spiritual abuse lurked in the shadows.** What I saw behind the scenes didn't line up with the Jesus I read about in Scripture. And what I endured at home—emotional torment, control, and cruelty—deepened the cracks in my soul. Eventually, the questions overwhelmed the answers.

And I walked away.

Before Google existed and long before YouTube theology was a thing, I spent hours at the library studying every belief system I had ever heard of, including the dark arts. **I was desperate for *truth***—what held up to scrutiny. But the more I searched, the more fragmented Christianity seemed. Doctrines contradicted each other. Interpretations competed. Everyone claimed to have the "real truth," but they couldn't even agree on baptism or be nice to their neighbor.

My faith didn't just unravel—**it deconstructed completely**. And before I knew it, I was light-years from the Gospel and deep in the occult as a full-on practicing Luciferian witch. For a decade, I chased what I thought was "hidden knowledge," convinced I had finally evolved beyond religious rules and into spiritual enlightenment. I openly mocked Christianity and believed I knew better through my personal lens of logic and reason.

Then one day, God ripped the scales from my eyes.

In a single, jarring moment, He revealed my fate. And what I saw was terrifying: the depth of my deception, the darkness I had welcomed, and the lies I had wrapped around my soul like armor. It wasn't empowerment. It was bondage and evil masquerading as freedom and light.

In that moment, **I knew I couldn't trust myself to make spiritual decisions**. I had followed every feeling, every intuition, every "inner knowing"—and it had led me straight into the hands of the evil one. I begged God to show me the way and not allow me to be deceived again. I was very cautious and moved forward slowly. I didn't follow my gut reactions; I prayed and follow God's lead. I wasn't interested in an emotional high or a casual Bible study. **I wanted authentic Christianity**. I asked Him to lead me—not to a denomination that made me feel good—but to **the** Church **He founded**. The one built on rock, not sand.

And He did.

He answered that prayer, not with flashing lights or burning bushes, but with evidence, history, Scripture, and the still, small voice that said:

Look again.

Dig deeper.

Keep going.

This book is the fruit of that search. It's not so much my story as it is the case for why I became convinced that the Church Jesus Christ established still exists today. Because **I wasn't looking to have my ears tickled or feelings appeased. I was looking for the real Jesus. The whole truth and nothing but the truth**. And when you follow the truth all the way to the end, you don't find an elusive idea, a well-spoken influencer, or a guru with a didgeridoo. **You find Christ**. And He is alive in His Church today.

Is There Really Only ONE True Church?

In a world filled with thousands of Christian denominations, countless preachers and teachers, and conflicting interpretations of Scripture and traditions, it's natural to ask: *How can we know which church is the one Jesus Himself established?* With so many voices claiming to speak for Christ, **how can we discern the true Church**—the one that teaches with **His authority** and continues His mission in the world?

Thankfully, Jesus did not leave us guessing. He established a **visible Church**, built on the foundation of the apostles, with a clear structure and sacramental life. And from the earliest centuries, Christians affirmed this unity and identity in a single, unifying declaration: *the Nicene Creed*. First formulated at the Council of Nicaea in 325 AD and completed at the Council of Constantinople in 381 AD, the Creed was designed to proclaim the true faith and to protect it from false teachings—especially those denying the divinity of Christ and the personhood of the Holy Spirit.

Far from being a relic of history, the Nicene Creed is a **roadmap for discerning the true Church**. It affirms belief in "**One, Holy, Catholic, and Apostolic Church**"—**four essential marks that help us identify the Church Jesus founded**. Not many churches but *one*. Not humanly invented but *divinely instituted and guided by the Holy Spirit*. This chapter will explore how the Creed offers not just theology, but clarity. And it will show why, even in the chaos of modern Christianity, we can still trace the straight line of truth back to the Church Christ built.

The Nicene Creed:

I believe in one God,
the Father almighty,
maker of heaven and earth,
of all things visible and invisible.

I believe in one Lord Jesus Christ,
the Only Begotten Son of God,
born of the Father before all ages.
God from God, Light from Light,
true God from true God,
begotten, not made, consubstantial with the Father;
through Him all things were made.
For us men and for our salvation
He came down from heaven,

and by the Holy Spirit was incarnate of the Virgin Mary,
and became man.

For our sake He was crucified under Pontius Pilate,
He suffered death and was buried,
and rose again on the third day
in accordance with the Scriptures.
He ascended into heaven
and is seated at the right hand of the Father.
He will come again in glory
to judge the living and the dead
and His Kingdom will have no end.

I believe in the Holy Spirit, the Lord, the giver of life,
who proceeds from the Father and the Son,
who with the Father and the Son is adored and glorified,
who has spoken through the prophets.

I believe in One, Holy, Catholic, and Apostolic Church.
I confess one Baptism for the forgiveness of sins
and I look forward to the resurrection of the dead
and the life of the world to come.

Amen.

If Jesus truly founded a Church—as He said He would in Matthew 16:18—then it matters profoundly which Church is the ONE He established. He did not leave us with vague spirituality like a bad life coach, some hippie guru, or even a book (more on this later), nor did He teach a personal relationship detached from a visible community. **He founded a real, visible Church built on the apostles, with divine authority to teach, sanctify, and govern in His name.** The Nicene Creed, professed by Christians since the fourth century, affirms that this Church is **"One, Holy, Catholic, and Apostolic."** These four marks are not romantic ideals—they are concrete identifiers that guide us in finding the true Church Jesus established.

Only the Catholic Church fully bears these four marks. It is **one**, maintaining unity in faith, Sacraments, and leadership under the Pope; **holy**, not because all members are perfect, but because it is divinely founded, has the saints, and dispenses grace through the Sacraments; **catholic**, meaning "universal," present across the globe and faithful to all Christ taught; and **apostolic**, with a direct line of succession from the apostles through the bishops. Protestant communities, though sincere, **were founded by men centuries later** and lack apostolic succession and doctrinal unity. If we believe Jesus keeps His promises, then we must seek the one Church He established—and that Church is the Catholic Church.

Let's investigate this more deeply and see how Catholicism is not only true but biblical.

"I had always believed that the early Church was Protestant. But when I actually studied the early Church Fathers,
I was shocked to discover that they were Catholic in their beliefs,
in their worship, and in their structure."

—Dr. Scott Hahn (former Calvinist & Presbyterian minister)

Apostolic Authority: Why It Matters

The Catholic Church makes a profound and audacious claim: that it is the one true Church founded by Jesus Christ. This isn't merely a pious tradition or a theological preference—**it is a declaration with eternal implications**. Either Jesus left us a visible, authoritative Church guided by His Spirit and protected from error, or we are left to the chaos of human interpretation and denominational division. The Catholic Church stands alone in tracing its leadership, teachings, and sacramental life all the way back to Christ and the apostles without interruption.

This claim is not blind or arrogant—**it's testable**. It's supported by Scripture, confirmed by the witness of history, and upheld through apostolic succession: the continuous handing on of authority from the apostles to today's bishops through the laying on of hands. **No other Christian body can credibly make that same historical and theological case**. While others may share in partial truths or elements of grace, only the Catholic Church can point to the **fullness of faith**, preserved and handed down as Christ intended.

To accept this claim means confronting some uncomfortable questions. Why are there hundreds to thousands of Christian denominations today, all interpreting the same Bible differently? Why does the early Church look so distinctly Catholic in its structure, worship, and sacraments? And most importantly, if Christ founded a Church to teach in His name with His authority, wouldn't it still exist today—united, visible, and consistent in doctrine? The Catholic Church says **yes**. And this chapter will explore why that answer is not only reasonable—but true.

Founded by Christ Himself in 33 AD

- Jesus states in Matthew 16:18:

  "You are Peter, and on this rock, I will build my Church, and the gates of hell shall not prevail against it."

The Catholic Church teaches this as Christ instituting Peter as the leader of His Church, giving him the "keys of the Kingdom" (divine authority). The idea that Peter was not merely "first among equals" but the authoritative leader of the Church is deeply rooted in both Scripture and Tradition. We'll break this down by examining his name change, his unique role in Scripture, and how the early Church (the first Christians, those who were taught by Christ Himself or by His apostles) understood his authority later.

Apostolic Succession

- **The Catholic bishops today are direct spiritual descendants of the apostles**—through the laying on of hands (ordination) passed down in an **unbroken line**. This isn't just symbolic—it's how the **authority** to teach, govern, and sanctify is transmitted through generations, fulfilling Jesus' promise:

  "He who hears you hears me."–Luke 10:16.

Early Church Fathers, such as St. Irenaeus (second century), affirmed this continuity, stating that the bishops, especially in Rome, inherited their authority from the apostles.

Scriptural Consistency

- The New Testament frequently speaks of a **visible, hierarchical Church** (e.g., Acts 1:20, Acts 15, 1 Timothy 3:15–"the Church of the living God, the pillar and foundation of truth").

- Christ gave authority to the apostles to teach, sanctify, and govern (e.g., Matthew 28:19–20, John 20:21–23).

The Early Church Fathers' Writings

- Early Christians, such as St. Ignatius of Antioch (d. 107 AD), referred to the "Catholic Church" as the one, unified body of Christ.

- St. Cyprian of Carthage (third century) wrote: "You cannot have God for your Father if you do not have the Church for your mother."

Historical Continuity

- The Catholic Church is the only Christian body that **has existed continuously since the time of Christ**.

- While Protestant denominations **didn't originate until the sixteenth century** and the Eastern Orthodox Churches formally split in 1054 AD, the Catholic Church traces its leadership directly to Peter and the apostles.

Authority and the Magisterium

- Christ gave the Church teaching authority through the apostles and their successors (the bishops and the Pope).

- The doctrines of the Church have remained consistent over time, even amidst doctrinal challenges.

What Is the Magisterium?

- The Magisterium is the **teaching authority** of the Catholic Church, given by Christ to the apostles and passed down through their successors—the Pope and the bishops in union with him.

"He who hears you hears me."–Luke 10:16

"Whatever you bind on earth shall be bound in heaven." –Matthew 16:19, 18:18

Why Does the Magisterium Exist?

Its purpose is to:

- Safeguard and interpret Sacred Scripture and Sacred Tradition faithfully.

- Ensure **unity and truth** in doctrine across all times and cultures.

- **Protect the Church** from error in faith and morals.

The Magisterium is not above the Word of God but serves it faithfully, under the guidance of the Holy Spirit.

Three Levels of Magisterial Teaching

1. **Extraordinary Magisterium**–Infallible definitions of doctrine by:

   ◦ Ecumenical Councils (e.g., Council of Nicaea, Trent, Vatican II)

   ◦ Ex cathedra statements by the Pope (e.g., Immaculate Conception in 1854)

2. **Ordinary Universal Magisterium**–Infallible teachings held consistently by all bishops in union with the Pope, even if not solemnly defined (e.g., male-only priesthood).

3. **Ordinary Magisterium**–Non-infallible teachings that still require religious assent, even if not defined infallibly.

Why We Need the Magisterium

Without the Magisterium, Christianity splinters—everyone becomes their own interpreter of Scripture (essentially, their own "pope"), which is why we see as many Protestant churches as there are opinions. This is also the root of why so many dangerous cults exist; **Scripture left to the individual interpretation of men, without the apostolic deposit of faith and protection of the Holy Spirit, often leads to the justification of abuse**. The Magisterium provides a living, Spirit-guided voice of Christ in His Church, ensuring that the faith remains One, Holy, Catholic, and Apostolic.

Conclusion: Christ's Authority Continues Through His Church

Jesus didn't come to leave us with vague ideas, personal opinions, or a do-it-yourself spirituality. He came in the flesh, established a Church, and entrusted that Church with His own divine authority to teach, govern, and sanctify. That's not just a Catholic assertion—it's a truth woven throughout Scripture.

When He told the apostles, "He who hears you, hears me" (Luke 10:16), He wasn't being poetic. He was giving them His voice. When He said, "As the Father has sent me, so I send you" (John 20:21), He wasn't talking about abstract spiritual inspiration—**He was commissioning them to carry out His mission visibly, sacramentally, and authoritatively**.

This is the incarnational reality of our faith: God works not just through thoughts or feelings, but through people, flesh, and history. Just as Christ became visible in the Incarnation, **He remains visible in His Church**, which Scripture calls His body (1 Corinthians 12:27). That's why the apostles laid hands on successors. That's why Paul could write, "We are ambassadors for Christ, God making His appeal through us" (2

Corinthians 5:20). That's why Church councils spoke with real authority—because Jesus promised to be with His Church always (Matthew 28:20), and the Holy Spirit would guide her into all truth (John 16:13).

To reject the Church's authority is not just to walk away from a religious institution—it's to walk away from the very authority of Christ, who speaks and acts through it. The Catholic Church doesn't take Jesus' place. She carries His mission. She is His hands and feet. She is His voice in the world.

This isn't about control. It's about communion. The Church's authority isn't a burden—it's a gift of love protected by truth. Just as a good father guards his family with wisdom and order, so too the Church protects the Gospel from error and guards us from the confusion of self-made religion.

Jesus didn't leave us to guess our way through life. He came to lead us home. And He gave us a Church to light the path—with His voice, His truth, and His authority.

By What Authority?
Why "Bible Alone" Isn't Biblical

The Protestant Reformation began with a bold rejection—Martin Luther's break from the Catholic Church in the sixteenth century was fueled by a rejection of the Pope's authority, the teaching authority of the Magisterium, and the weight of **Sacred Tradition**. In doing so, Luther severed ties with the very Church Christ established and introduced a radical new principle: *Sola Scriptura*—the idea that Scripture alone is the sole rule of faith. **But who gave Martin Luther the authority to change what had been for over 1500 years? And what happens when each person becomes their own final authority on interpreting the Bible?**

Division.

For over 1500 years, **the idea that individuals could interpret Scripture apart from the Church was unheard of.** Early Christians relied on Sacred Tradition and the teaching authority of the bishops, who were successors of the apostles. There was no such thing as "Bible alone" theology. The Church was the custodian of both Scripture and its proper interpretation. It wasn't until the Reformation that individuals began treating the Bible as a self-interpreting manual—detached from the Church that canonized it. **No Christian in the first fifteen centuries believed in Sola Scriptura**. The concept simply did not exist. And without a unified voice to **safeguard and interpret Scripture**, Protestantism began to fracture almost immediately. Even during Luther's own lifetime, fellow Reformers like Ulrich Zwingli, John Calvin, and the Anabaptists **disagreed with him on fundamental doctrines**: the nature of the Eucharist, the role of baptism, predestination, and the structure of the Church itself. What was once a movement claiming to restore unity and purity of doctrine quickly became a **fragmented web of competing interpretations**—each one claiming to follow "just the Bible," yet arriving at drastically different conclusions.

The result?

Today there are hundreds to tens of thousands of Protestant denominations, each built on a **different interpretation** of the same sacred text. Protestants have essentially created their own "popes" without any centralized apostolic authority or binding doctrine—just thousands of people determining what scripture means through their own thoughts, feelings, and opinions. **This chaos is not the fruit of the Holy Spirit, who brings unity—not confusion** (1 Corinthians 14:33). Jesus prayed that His followers would be *one* (John 17:21), **not divided by personal opinions or doctrinal disagreement**. This chapter will explore the roots and ripple effects of *Sola Scriptura*, and why the rejection of the Church's teaching authority has led not to freedom—but to fragmentation.

A Closer Look at Martin Luther

The founder of Protestantism, Martin Luther, is often portrayed as a courageous reformer standing up against a corrupt Church. While it's true that abuses existed in the sixteenth century (more on this later), what is often left out of modern accounts is the darker, more troubling side of Luther's life, writings, and **motivations**.

Luther was deeply afflicted by what appears to have been **scrupulosity**, a form of religious obsessive-compulsive disorder that left him tormented by fears of damnation and divine wrath. Even as a monk, he confessed obsessively—sometimes multiple times a day—terrified he had forgotten to mention a single sin. His spiritual torment likely **distorted his view of God** from a loving Father into a harsh judge. When a person views God in this way, **any system of grace mediated**

through the Church can begin to look like manipulation rather than mercy. His rejection of Church authority, the Sacraments, and ultimately the papacy may have had more to do with his **inner turmoil** than divine inspiration.

Moreover, **Luther's own writings**—often ignored today—**betray a spirit that was anything but holy**. In his infamous work *On the Jews and Their Lies* (1543), he spewed virulent anti-Semitism, calling for the burning of synagogues, the destruction of Jewish homes, and the confiscation of their property. **These writings were later used by the Nazis as ideological justification for their atrocities**. He also wrote with similar contempt toward the disabled and those he considered mentally deficient, saying such people were possessed by the devil or useless to society. **These are not the words of a man governed by charity or humility**.

Luther also spread **false claims about the Church's teachings on indulgences**, suggesting they were being "sold for salvation." While some abuses occurred in isolated areas, the Church never taught that salvation could be bought. **An indulgence is not a pardon for sin** but a remission of the temporal punishment due to sin—something granted **by the authority** Christ gave the Church (Matthew 16:19). Even the Ninety-five Theses themselves were written in Latin and originally intended for academic debate—not the revolution they sparked. And even if certain clergy were corrupt or poorly catechized, **the sins of a few priests do not invalidate the truth of the Sacraments, or the authority of the Church Christ founded**.

In the end, **Luther didn't purify the Church—he fractured it**. His personal spiritual struggles, toxic writings, and disdain for ecclesial authority set in motion a division that would splinter Christendom into tens of thousands of conflicting denominations. This seems more in line with the devil's agenda than a holy reform. **The irony is stark**: in attempting to escape a Church he saw as broken, he created a system with no central authority, no consistent doctrine, and, ultimately, no unity.

The Reformation was not a return to apostolic truth—it was a **rebellion** born of misunderstanding, pain, and **pride**. The answer to corruption is not chaos. The answer to bad priests is not abandoning the Church but reforming it from within, **as the saints have always done**.

Clarification on Indulgences:

Martin Luther's original objection was **not against indulgences themselves** but against the **abuse** of indulgences by a **small group** of clergy in **Germany**—particularly the misleading claim that indulgences could *forgive sins* or *guarantee salvation*, which was **never** official Church teaching.

Luther actually **agreed with legitimate indulgences**. In his **Ninety-five Theses (#71)**, he wrote that anyone who speaks against the Church's teaching on indulgences should be **anathema** (cursed). The real issue was **local abuse**—often by poorly trained priests.

After the Black Death (1300s), **Europe had a major shortage of priests**, leading to **mass ordinations** without proper theological training. Many priests simply didn't understand indulgences correctly. Church authorities themselves were already aware of abuses. The Fifth Lateran Council (1512–1517), just before Luther's protest, had called for **reform** of indulgence practices. So you see, the Church in her wisdom had already begun her own "reformation" to address this long before Luther's rebellious revolt. But because one man put himself above the established authority of God, we now have as many churches as there are opinions.

Doctrinal Chaos: The Famous "30,000 Protestant Denominations" Claim

To be fair, let's address the supposed "tens of thousands" of Protestant denominations claim, generally made by Catholics. This number comes from the **World Christian Encyclopedia** (WCE), particularly the editions published by David Barrett and later by the Center for the Study of Global Christianity. In the **2001 edition**, they cited:

- **Over 33,000 denominations worldwide,**

- Of which **approximately 26,000 were Protestant** or "independent" groups stemming from the Reformation.

What Counts As a "Denomination"?

Here's the catch:

- The WCE counts a "denomination" not just by doctrine, but **by geography and governance**, too.

- So, if **Baptists in Nigeria** and **Baptists in Brazil** are organized separately, they count as *two denominations*, even if their theology is basically the same.

This is why critics (especially Protestants) say the number is inflated.

The More Conservative Approach

If you only count **major distinct Protestant traditions** (like Baptist, Pentecostal, Lutheran, Presbyterian, Anglican, Methodist, etc.), then you're probably looking at **hundreds**, not tens of thousands.

But if you count every **independent church movement**, every **non-denominational network**, and every **splinter group**, then the **30,000+ figure** becomes much more understandable—even **understated**—today.

In the **2023 edition of the WCE,** the number has climbed closer to **45,000–50,000 Protestant and independent groups.**

So what's the *real* answer?

Both are true, depending on how you define "denomination":

- **Doctrinally distinct major branches?** → ~200–300

- **All independently organized Protestant/independent churches worldwide?** → 30,000–50,000+

The bottom line is that there is undeniable fragmentation in Protestantism compared to the **One, Holy, Catholic, and Apostolic Church** Christ established. Even if we go with the conservative number, the point remains:

Protestantism is characterized by **division,** while Catholicism has maintained **doctrinal unity** for over 2,000 years.

So, with that said, there are hundreds, if not thousands, of Protestant denominations—each claiming to teach the Bible "correctly," yet often **contradicting** one another.

- Some baptize infants, others don't.

- Some believe the Eucharist is symbolic, others believe Jesus is present but deny that it's truly His presence in Body, Blood, Soul and Divinity, as the early church taught.

- Some accept contraception, abortion, and same-sex marriage, others don't.

Whose interpretation is right? Who has the authority to say?

The truth is: **without the Church, everyone becomes their own Pope.**

From Doctrine to Preference

This lack of authority has led many Protestant churches to adapt their services to personal preferences and modern trends, rather than **divine worship**.

Common features:

- Cool music designed to evoke emotion rather than *reverence*.

- Motivational sermons that sound more like TED Talks than the Gospel.

- A focus on "what God can do for you" rather than worshiping what God has already done on the Cross.

Christ is often reduced to a life coach, and instead of the Mass—a sacred mystery in the early Church—"worship" becomes a concert + lecture combo with coffee and donuts in the lobby. This isn't to say that motivational talks, biblical discussions, and even emotional music are in and of themselves "bad." They can have their place in the Christian life. But **on the Lord's Day we are to worship Him in spirit and truth,** and this simply is not proper sacred worship.

Praise, honor, and glory? Yes. But not sacrificial worship. (We'll dive more into this later.)

Language and definitions matter. We don't get to create our own truth, despite the culture we live in today saying so.

Christianity Without the Cross

Many modern churches preach comfort, success, and feelings rather than repentance, sacrifice, and holiness.

- The early Christians faced persecution, suffering, and martyrdom—but they were sustained by the **Eucharist, the Sacraments,**

and the apostolic faith.

- Today, many people seek a church that "feels right," where they enjoy the music and the preaching and are entertained, rather than seeking one that is **true**.

But truth doesn't change based on feelings or popularity. It rests on the **authority** Christ gave to His Church. This isn't to say our feelings aren't important, but our mind and emotions can be **easily manipulated** by the adversary, especially when we're outside of the protection of the Church through the Sacraments.

Why the Catholic Church Has Authority

Jesus didn't leave us with just a book. He left us a Church, with real authority:

> "You are Peter, and on this rock I will build my Church… I give you the keys of the Kingdom" (Matthew 16:18–19).

The Catholic Church has:

- Apostolic succession from Peter to the Pope.

- The Magisterium, guided by the Holy Spirit, to preserve the faith.

- The Sacraments, instituted by Christ, to give grace.

Priestly Ordination vs. Protestant Pastors "Calling"

This comparison really highlights the depth, rigor, and apostolic structure of the Catholic priesthood versus the flexible, often informal approach of many non-denominational Protestant pastors:

Vocation and Formation Comparison

Category	Catholic Priest	Average Protestant/Non-Denominational Pastor
Formation	Years of discernment; 6–8 years of seminary training in philosophy, theology, Scripture, Church history, pastoral ministry; ordained in apostolic succession.	No standardized path; may attend Bible college for 2–4 years, or none; training ranges from thorough to minimal; recognized by local congregation, network, or denomination.
Theological Foundation	Rooted in Sacred Scripture, Sacred Tradition, and the Magisterium; unified theology developed and safeguarded over 2,000 years; must defend doctrines like Eucharist, Trinity, Marian dogmas.	Typically taught *Sola Scriptura*; theology based on personal or popular authors' interpretations; major variations in doctrine across churches (baptism, Eucharist, salvation, etc.).
Authority and Accountability	Acts in persona Christi during Sacraments; accountable to a bishop in apostolic succession; bound by canon law and Church hierarchy; cannot invent or change doctrine.	Often independent or loosely affiliated; accountable mainly to a board or congregation; free to preach based on personal interpretation; no apostolic succession.
Role in Worship and Sacraments	Celebrates the Holy Sacrifice of the Mass; administers all seven Sacraments; spiritual father, confessor, and teacher by the authority of Christ through apostolic succession and proper ordination.	Leads worship services centered on music and preaching; may offer symbolic communion or baptism; focuses mainly on teaching and leadership without sacramental ministry.

Conclusion: Protestantism—The Real "Traditions of Men"

- **Jesus founded the Catholic Church (Matthew 16:18–19, John 21:17).**

- **Men**—Luther, Calvin, Henry VIII—**founded Protestant denominations 1,500 years later**, each teaching different, contradictory doctrines, and all based on their own personal agenda.

The Protestant Reformation did not restore Christian unity; it shattered it. Martin Luther's rebellion against the authority of the Church Christ founded led to **doctrinal chaos and confusion**—exactly what **Scripture warns against,** for *"God is not a God of confusion but of peace"* (1 Corinthians 14:33). By placing personal interpretation above the authority of the Church, the Reformers opened the floodgates to endless divisions. Today, the thousands of Protestant denominations, each contradicting the others while claiming to follow "just the Bible," are the inevitable **fruit of that rebellion.** Jesus prayed that His followers would be one (John 17:21), yet Protestantism has multiplied disunity, not preserved it.

Upon This Rock:
The Biblical Foundations of the Papacy

Modern Christians often overlook a crucial truth: Jesus was a faithful, practicing Second Temple Israelite Jew. He didn't arrive in a vacuum or invent a brand-new religion out of thin air. For a first-century Jew, the Catholic Church would not appear as a break from their sacred traditions but as their fulfillment. **Jesus did not abolish the law—He fulfilled it** (Matthew 5:17)—and He established a New Covenant that retained the essence of Jewish worship: priesthood, sacrifice, liturgy, and authority. **The early Church didn't discard structure; it inherited and elevated it**. Just as the Israelites had a visible priesthood, sacred rituals, and hierarchical leadership, the Church preserves these in their **perfected form** through the Sacraments, apostolic succession, and the teaching authority of the Magisterium. Rather than reducing faith to a private, unstructured buffet of beliefs, the Catholic Church continues the **covenant model**—a family of God with order, worship, and Sacred Tradition, just as God always intended.

To understand the papacy, we need to recognize typology.

Typology is the study of how certain people, events, and institutions in the Old Testament serve as a **foreshadowing—or "type"—of greater realities fulfilled in the New Testament**. These types are like divine previews, intentionally woven into salvation history by God to prepare His people for Christ and His Church. For example, Adam is a type of Christ, the "new Adam" who brings life instead of death (Romans 5:14). The Passover lamb prefigures Jesus, the true Lamb of God. The manna in the wilderness foreshadows the Eucharist, the Bread of Life. These are not coincidences—they are part of God's consistent pattern of revelation, where the Old prepares the way for the New, and the New fulfills the promises of the Old.

The entire structure of salvation history is deeply rooted in the Jewish tradition, and **if we fail to understand those roots, we risk missing the richness and depth of what Christ actually established.**

This is especially true when it comes to the papacy. For many, the idea of a Pope—a single visible head of the Church—feels foreign, unnecessary, or even man-made. But Scripture and history tell a different story. In fact, the very concept of a prime minister or royal steward, entrusted with the king's authority and acting in his name, **was already established in the Old Testament**. This role was called the *Al Bayit*, or "Over the House," a position within the Davidic Kingdom that held the keys of authority when the king was absent. Sound familiar?

Jesus, the Son of David, established a Kingdom—not some esoteric spiritualism, but a real, structured, authoritative Church. And in doing so, **He echoed the same structure that the Jews would have recognized: a king, a covenant, and a prime minister to manage the household.** In Matthew 16, when Jesus gives Peter the "keys of the Kingdom," He's not inventing a new symbol. He's fulfilling a very old one. The papacy, then, isn't a later invention—it's the natural and supernatural continuation of a biblical office, transformed and elevated by Christ for the New Covenant. This chapter will trace those Jewish roots and show how the role of the Pope is deeply and intentionally woven into the fabric of salvation history.

Peter as the Fulfillment of the Davidic Steward

- In Isaiah 22:20–22, God appoints Eliakim as the Al Bayit (chief steward) under the Davidic king. The passage states:

  "I will place on his shoulder the key of the house of David; what he opens no one can shut, and what he shuts no one can open."

27

- **This is directly echoed in Matthew 16:18–19**, where Jesus gives Peter the keys of the Kingdom of Heaven, using nearly identical language:

  "I will give you the keys of the Kingdom of Heaven; whatever you bind on earth shall be bound in heaven, and whatever you loose on earth shall be loosed in heaven."

  This "key" was a **symbol of authority**, given to the steward who acted on behalf of the king—kind of like a prime minister in a monarchy. The steward wasn't the king, but he exercised the king's authority **in his absence**, managing the kingdom and ensuring stability.

The Davidic Kingdom as a Model for the Church

- The Davidic Kingdom had a visible, hierarchical structure, which Jesus, as the Son of David (Matthew 1:1), reestablished in His Church.

- Just as the Al Bayit governed the king's household, the Pope (as Peter's successor) governs Christ's household, the Church.

He's appointing Peter to a fulfillment of that same office—a royal steward in the new, eternal Kingdom. This isn't just about leadership; it's about a divinely established office that carries real, binding authority (as Jesus continues: "whatever you bind on earth shall be bound in heaven…").

Just as Eliakim was a visible representative of the Davidic king, Peter becomes the visible head of Christ's Church on earth—a role that continues in the papacy today.

A Strong Argument—Though Not Without Debate

To be fair, some biblical scholars—especially those outside the Catholic tradition—question the strength of this typological connection. They argue that while the imagery may be similar, it doesn't *prove* that Jesus was instituting a continuing office of papal authority.

However, even among non-Catholic scholars, there is often recognition that the **allusion to Isaiah 22 is deliberate** and meaningful. And within Catholic theology, this typology is not offered as a stand-alone proof but as part of a **broader biblical and historical argument** that includes apostolic succession, the early Church's understanding of Peter's primacy, and the ongoing need for visible unity and authority.

So while not everyone agrees on its full implications, the Eliakim connection remains a rich and theologically consistent argument—one that strengthens the case for the papacy by rooting it deeply in the Davidic Kingdom Jesus came to fulfill.

Peter's Name Change: Cephas (Kepha) and Its Meaning

- In John 1:42, Jesus renames Simon:

  "You are Simon son of John; you will be called Cephas" (which is translated as Peter).

- Cephas (*Kepha* in Aramaic) means "rock."

- In Matthew 16:18, Jesus confirms this change:

  "You are Peter (*Petros*), and on this rock (*Petra*) I will build my Church."

- Name changes in Scripture signify a divine mission:

  - **Abram** → Abraham (Genesis 17:5) to become the father of nations.

- ○ **Jacob** → Israel (Genesis 32:28) to lead God's chosen people.

- ○ **Simon** → Peter to be the foundation of Christ's Church.

Why Is This Important?

- Jesus could have called him "little stone" (*lithos* in Greek) but instead called him "rock" (*kepha* in Aramaic).

- In biblical thought, a rock represents stability, permanence, and a foundation—not mere primacy among equals.

Peter Speaks for the Apostles

- Matthew 16:16–Peter declares Jesus as the Messiah, and Jesus blesses him.

- John 6:68–69–After many disciples leave Jesus, Peter alone speaks for the Twelve:

  "Lord, to whom shall we go? You have the words of eternal life."

- Acts 1:15–26–Peter takes the lead in choosing Judas's replacement.

- Acts 2:14–41–Peter gives the first public sermon at Pentecost.

Peter's Name Appears First and Most Often

- The Twelve Apostles are listed multiple times in the Gospels, and Peter is always first (Matthew 10:2, Mark 3:16, Luke 6:14).

- Even when only three apostles are mentioned (Peter, James, and John), **Peter is always first**.

- In contrast, **Judas Iscariot is always last** in these lists.

Peter as the Chief Shepherd (Not Just a Spokesman)

- In John 21:15–17, after the Resurrection, Jesus asks Peter three times:

- "Simon, son of John, do you love Me?"

- "Feed My lambs… Tend My sheep… Feed My sheep."

- Jesus is not just forgiving Peter's denial—**He is giving him authority over the flock.**

- The words "feed" and "tend" (*bosko* and *poimaino* in Greek) are pastoral terms, showing Peter is the **chief shepherd** under Christ.

The Early Church Recognized Peter's Leadership

- Acts 15:7–12–At the Council of Jerusalem, there was much debate, but Peter stood up and declared the final decision, which was then affirmed by James.

- Church Fathers Affirm Peter's Authority:

  - **St. Ignatius of Antioch** (c. 110 AD) calls the Roman Church "the one that presides in love."

  - **St. Irenaeus** (c. 180 AD) says all churches must be in agreement with the Church of Rome, founded by Peter.

  - **St. Cyprian** (third century) writes that Peter was given the "primacy" so that the Church would remain one and undivided.

In Acts 5:15, we read that people "carried the sick out into the streets and laid them on beds and mats so that **at least Peter's shadow might fall on some of them as he passed by.**" This striking detail reveals the unique spiritual authority and grace that surrounded Peter, **distinguishing him** among the apostles. No other apostle's shadow is

31

mentioned this way. It mirrors how in the Old Testament, objects connected to prophets could carry divine power—not by magic, but by God's choice to work through certain individuals. **This passage underscores the primacy and visible leadership role Peter held** in the early Church, consistent with his being named the "rock" in Matthew 16 and entrusted with the keys to the Kingdom. It supports the idea that **Peter's office was distinct**—and divinely appointed—laying the foundation for the ongoing leadership of the papacy.

Conclusion: Peter Was More than First Among Equals

When we look at the big picture, it becomes clear that Peter wasn't just one apostle among many. Jesus gave him a unique mission—He even changed his name to **"rock,"** something God only does when someone is being given a special role in salvation history. Peter is the only one Jesus gave the **keys to the Kingdom**, and throughout the New Testament, Peter consistently steps into that leadership role.

Jesus didn't say, "Let's all lead equally." He told Peter specifically to **"feed My sheep"**—to shepherd the flock. That's not just symbolic language. It's a real assignment of spiritual leadership. And the early Church recognized this. When major decisions were made, when unity was needed, **they looked to Rome—Peter's see—as the center of Christian authority**.

This isn't just tradition—it's **biblical, historical, and deeply rooted in how Christ chose to build His Church.** The role of the Pope isn't an invention of the Middle Ages. It's the continuation of the very structure Jesus set in place when He handed the keys to Peter. To learn more on this topic, see Brant Pitre's *Jesus and the Jewish Roots of the Papacy*, Joe Heschmeyer's *Pope Peter*, and Erick Ybarra's, *The Roots of the Papacy: The Patristic Logic*.

Hidden in Plain Sight:
What the Scriptures Reveal About Mary

To understand Mary's role in salvation history, we must return once again to the Jewish roots of the Christian faith. Mary isn't just a figure of piety or a gentle presence in nativity scenes—her role is deeply theological, profoundly biblical, and firmly rooted in the traditions of ancient Israel. Far from being an optional add-on to Christianity, Mary is an essential part of God's divine blueprint, **prepared from the beginning and revealed in fullness through her "yes" to God.**

In the Davidic Kingdom, the queen was not the king's wife—it was his **mother.** This position was known as the *Gebirah,* or "Great Lady," and she held a unique and powerful role: **she sat beside the king, interceded on behalf of the people, and was honored with royal dignity.** This tradition helps us understand why, in the New Covenant, the mother of the King—Jesus—would also hold a distinct and exalted place. Mary's role as the Queen Mother doesn't diminish Christ's authority; it **magnifies His kingship.** After all, no one threatens the king's glory more than a rival—but no one highlights it more than a Queen Mother enthroned at His side.

Mary is also revealed in Scripture as the true Ark of the New Covenant. Just as the original Ark carried the stone tablets of the law, the manna from heaven, and the priestly rod of Aaron, Mary carried within her womb the Word made flesh, the Bread of Life, and the Eternal High Priest. The Old Testament Ark was overshadowed by the glory of God—so was Mary at the Annunciation. **These aren't mere coincidences; they are divine fulfillments.** This chapter will explore how Mary, in her unique role, brings Old Testament symbols to life and serves as a living bridge between the covenants—chosen by God, honored by heaven, and given to us as a spiritual mother.

Mary as the Gebirah (Queen Mother)

- In the Davidic Kingdom, the king's mother, not his wife, held the royal title of Queen Mother (Gebirah).

- The Queen Mother had intercessory authority and was honored by the king (see 1 Kings 2:19, where Solomon bows before his mother Bathsheba).

- In Luke 1:32–33, the angel Gabriel announces that Jesus will inherit David's throne, implying that His mother would be the Gebirah of the Messianic Kingdom.

- This explains why Mary is honored and intercedes for believers, as seen at the Wedding at Cana (John 2:1–11).

Mary as the New Ark of the Covenant

- The Ark of the Covenant in the Old Testament held:

    1. The Word of God (Ten Commandments)

    2. The Manna (heavenly bread)

    3. Aaron's priestly staff

- In the New Testament, Mary carried:

    1. Jesus, the Word made flesh (John 1:14)

    2. The Bread of Life (John 6:35)

    3. The Eternal High Priest (Hebrews 4:14)

- The parallels between 2 Samuel 6 (where David brings the Ark to

Jerusalem) and Luke 1:39–56 (Mary visiting Elizabeth) reinforce this connection:

- ◦ The Ark stayed in the house of Obed-Edom for three months (2 Samuel 6:11), while Mary stayed with Elizabeth for three months (Luke 1:56).

- ◦ David leaped before the Ark (2 Samuel 6:16), just as John the Baptist leaped in Elizabeth's womb (Luke 1:44).

- Revelation 11:19–12:1 explicitly links the Ark with the "woman clothed with the sun," whom Catholics identify as Mary.

The title "Mary as the New Eve" is deeply rooted in Scripture and the writings of the early Church Fathers. Just as Jesus is the New Adam (Romans 5:12–21, 1 Corinthians 15:45), Mary is the New Eve, playing a crucial role in the reversal of the Fall.

The First Eve vs. The New Eve

The connection between Eve and Mary is seen in how their actions influence salvation history:

First Eve	New Eve (Mary)
• Created without sin	• Conceived without sin (Immaculate Conception)
• A virgin	• A virgin
• Disobeyed God	• Obeyed God perfectly
• Listened to a fallen angel (Satan)	• Listened to a faithful angel (Gabriel)
• Brought sin into the world through her disobedience	• Brought salvation into the world through her obedience
• Caused Adam to sin, leading to death	• Cooperated with the New Adam (Jesus), leading to life

Eve's disobedience brought death to the world, while Mary's obedience brought forth the Savior of the world.

Genesis 3:15–The First Prophecy of Mary

- After the Fall, God speaks to the serpent (Satan) in Genesis 3:15, known as the Protoevangelium (First Gospel):

  "I will put enmity between you and the woman, and between your offspring and hers; he will strike your head, and you will strike his heel."

- Who is "the woman"?

  ○ In the immediate context, it refers to Eve.

  ○ In its prophetic fulfillment, the "woman" is Mary, the mother of the Messiah.

  ○ This is confirmed in Revelation 12:1, where Mary appears as the "woman clothed with the sun."

"He will crush your head" → Mary's Role in Defeating Satan

- The prophecy foretells that a woman and her offspring (Jesus) will ultimately defeat Satan.

- Since Eve played a key role in the Fall, God ordained that another woman—Mary—would play a key role in Redemption.

- By bearing Christ, Mary brings forth the One who crushes Satan's power.

HIDDEN IN PLAIN SIGHT: WHAT THE SCRIPTURES REVEAL ABOUT MARY

Mary's Fiat: The Undoing of Eve's Disobedience

- When the angel Gabriel announces God's plan, Mary responds with perfect obedience:

  "Let it be done to me according to your word" (Luke 1:38).

- This is the exact opposite of Eve's disobedience in the Garden of Eden.

- St. Irenaeus (c. 180 AD), one of the earliest Church Fathers, wrote:

  "The knot of Eve's disobedience was untied by Mary's obedience. What the virgin Eve bound through her unbelief, the Virgin Mary loosened by her faith." (*Against Heresies*, 3.22.4)

- Just as Eve's "no" led to death, Mary's "yes" (Fiat) opened the door to eternal life.

The Wedding at Cana–The Woman Who Intercedes

- In John 2:1–11, at the Wedding at Cana, Jesus performs His first miracle at Mary's request.

- He calls her "Woman," just as Eve was originally called "Woman" in Genesis.

- This is not a sign of disrespect—Jesus is identifying Mary as the prophetic Woman of Genesis 3:15.

  - Mary's intercession at Cana parallels Eve's role in the Fall:

  - Eve influenced Adam to disobey → leading to death.

  - Mary influences Jesus to begin His ministry → leading to life.

Revelation 12: Mary as the Woman Clothed with the Sun

- Revelation 12:1 describes:

37

"A great sign appeared in heaven: a woman clothed with the sun, with the moon under her feet, and a crown of twelve stars on her head."

- This woman gives birth to the male child (Jesus), who will "rule all nations."

- She is in direct conflict with the ancient serpent, fulfilling Genesis 3:15.

- Just as Eve was the mother of all the living, Mary is the mother of all who have new life in Christ (John 19:26–27).

The Early Church Fathers on Mary as the New Eve

Many of the early Christians recognized Mary as the New Eve:

- St. Justin Martyr (c. 160 AD):

"Eve, while still a virgin, had conceived the word of the serpent and bore disobedience and death. But Mary, also a virgin, received faith and joy when the angel Gabriel announced the good news." (Dialogue with Trypho, 100)

- St. Irenaeus (c. 180 AD):

"Just as Eve was led to disobey God, so Mary was led to obey God, that the Virgin Mary might become the advocate of the virgin Eve." (*Against Heresies*, 5.19.1)

- **Tertullian** (c. 200 AD):

"Eve believed the serpent; Mary believed Gabriel. That which the one destroyed by believing, the other, by believing, set straight." (De Carne Christi, 17)

Conclusion: Mary's Important Role in Salvation History

Eve's disobedience ushered sin into the world, but **Mary's obedience opened the door to Redemption**. From the very beginning, this was foretold. In Genesis 3:15, God prophesied the coming of a woman whose offspring would crush the head of the serpent—a prophecy ultimately fulfilled through Mary, who brought forth Christ, the Savior who defeats Satan.

Mary's "yes" to God at the Annunciation reversed Eve's "no" in the Garden. In doing so, she became the New Eve, just as Jesus is the New Adam. **The connection is not accidental**. Jesus explicitly refers to His mother as "Woman" in both John 2 and John 19, echoing the language of Genesis and signaling Mary's unique role in salvation history.

The early Church Fathers unanimously recognized Mary in this light. Her cooperation with God's plan did not end with giving birth to the Messiah—it set in motion the healing of what had been broken at the Fall. Just as Jesus restores what Adam lost, Mary helps restore what Eve damaged by bringing Christ, the source of new life, into the world.

Both the Papacy and Mary's role in the Church **are not theological add-ons**—they are deeply rooted in the Jewish foundations of the faith. The Davidic Kingdom gives us the blueprint for the hierarchical nature of the Church, while Mary's identity as the Queen Mother and the New Ark of the Covenant reveals her unparalleled dignity in God's plan.

To explore these truths further, I highly recommend Scott Hahn's *Hail, Holy Queen* and Brant Pitre's *Jesus and the Jewish Roots of Mary*. These works beautifully unpack what the Church has always taught: Mary's role is not a distraction from Christ—it is a profound testimony to Him.

Where Did the Bible Come From?

For many Christians today, the Bible seems like the starting point of the faith—complete, bound, and ready to be opened. But few stop to ask *where* the Bible came from. Who preserved the writings? Who determined which books belonged? And under what **authority** were these decisions made? The answer might surprise you: **it was the Catholic Church, guided by the Holy Spirit, that safeguarded, discerned, and canonized the Scriptures we now call the Bible.**

The early Church did not begin with a Bible in hand. **In fact, for the first few centuries of Christianity, there was no universally recognized list of inspired books.** Christians relied on Sacred Tradition—the lived and taught faith passed down orally from the apostles—as well as letters, Gospels, and teachings read aloud during worship. As St. Paul said in 2 Thessalonians 2:15, "Hold fast to the traditions you were taught, whether by word of mouth or by letter." Both Scripture and tradition were seen as authoritative and inseparable, not competing sources of truth.

It wasn't until the late fourth century that the canon of Scripture was formally recognized, during councils such as Rome (382), Hippo (393), and Carthage (397), all under the authority of the Catholic Church. These councils didn't invent Scripture—they identified and confirmed what had already been used in the liturgy and affirmed by apostolic tradition. **The Church, which existed before the New Testament was compiled, acted as the instrument of discernment. In short, without the Catholic Church, we would not have the Bible as we know it today.** This chapter will unpack how the Bible came to be, and why trusting its authority ultimately points back to the Church that compiled it.

The Old Testament: Preserving the Septuagint

- By the time of Jesus, there were two major Jewish Scriptures in circulation:
    - **The Hebrew canon** (later formalized by Jewish leaders in the second century).
    - **The Greek Septuagint**, which included books like Wisdom, Sirach, Baruch, 1 & 2 Maccabees, Tobit, and Judith (now called the "Deuterocanonical" books).
- Jesus and the apostles quoted from the Septuagint, not just the Hebrew canon (e.g., Matthew 21:16, Hebrews 10:5-7).
- **The early Christians used the Septuagint**, which is why the Catholic Old Testament includes these books. The Protestants switched to using the Hebrew canon of the Jews, who rejected Christ! Why would we trust or want to use their scriptures over what Christians already formally canonized and had been using for over 1500 years?

The New Testament: Written by Catholics, for Catholics

- The New Testament books were written by Catholic bishops, apostles, and their disciples.
- The Gospels and Epistles were written within the Church, for the Church, and preserved by the Church.
- 2 Thessalonians 2:15:

"Hold fast to the traditions that you were taught, **whether by word of mouth** (passed down oral tradition) or by letter."

- This shows that **Scripture and Tradition were intertwined** and not to be separated.

The Church Determined the Canon

- The early Church had many Christian writings, including:

  ◦ The four Gospels (Matthew, Mark, Luke, John)

  ◦ Paul's letters

  ◦ Other letters (Peter, John, James, Jude)

  ◦ Other writings like the Shepherd of Hermas and Gospel of Thomas, which were later rejected.

- The Catholic Church, guided by the Holy Spirit, determined which books were divinely inspired.

- Key moments in defining the canon:

  ◦ **Synod of Rome** (382 AD)–Pope Damasus I confirmed the canon.

  ◦ **Councils of Hippo** (393 AD) & Carthage (397 AD)–The final seventy-three-book Bible was confirmed.

  ◦ **Council of Trent** (1546 AD)–Officially reaffirmed the canon in response to Protestant challenges.

The Church Preserved the Bible for Centuries

- For 1,500 years before the printing press, Catholic monks hand-copied the Bible in monasteries.

- The Church defended the Bible against heresies, ensuring its accurate transmission.

- The first complete Bible in Latin, the Vulgate, was translated by St. Jerome (fourth century) and became the standard for centuries.

Catholics Didn't "Add Books to the Bible"—Protestants *Removed* Them

The Protestant Old Testament is missing **seven** books found in the original Bible: *Tobit, Judith, Wisdom, Sirach (Ecclesiasticus), Baruch, and 1 & 2 Maccabees*, plus parts of *Daniel* and *Esther*. These are called the **Deuterocanonical books.**

These books were:

- Part of the **Septuagint**, the Greek Old Testament **widely used by Jews—including Jesus and the Apostles.**

- Quoted or alluded to in the New Testament (e.g., Hebrews 11:35 alludes to 2 Maccabees 7).

- **Accepted as Scripture by early Christians and Church Fathers.**

The early Church councils (Hippo in 393, Carthage in 397) **affirmed the canon including these books.** The Deuterocanon was **reaffirmed** at the **Council of Trent (1546)** in response to the Reformers' rejection of them.

Protestants Removed Books from the Bible

- In the 1500s, Martin Luther rejected the Deuterocanonical books because they contradicted some of his beliefs. **He put his own authority above God's Church and apostolic authority.**

- Luther also wanted to remove James, Hebrews, and Revelation but was persuaded to keep them.

- The Catholic Church kept the full Bible intact, as it had been for over a thousand years.

To be fair, Martin Luther did not immediately remove the Deuterocanonical books from the Bible. In his 1534 German translation, Luther **moved** these books into a separate section labeled "Apocrypha," calling them "books which are not held equal to the Holy Scriptures but are useful and good to read." While Luther still printed the books, **he undermined their authority in the minds of his followers**, planting seeds of doubt that would later result in their total removal from Protestant Bibles.

However, the deeper history is even more revealing.

Initially, Luther had no major problem with the Deuterocanonical books. But this changed **after he lost a key theological debate** where his opponent used **2 Maccabees** to defend Catholic doctrines, particularly **prayers for the dead** (2 Maccabees 12:44–46). The Catholic theologian **Johann Eck** referenced the Maccabean passage during the **Leipzig Debate (1519)** to counter Luther's arguments.

Rather than rethinking his theology, Luther **dismissed the authority of Maccabees**—and later the entire Deuterocanon—**to avoid having to address uncomfortable Catholic doctrines** like purgatory, prayers for the dead, and the intercession of saints.

Thus, Luther's rejection of these books was not driven by evidence of their falsity but by the fact that they contradicted his new theological positions. His solution was not to conform his doctrine to Scripture but to **change the contents of Scripture** itself.

Following Luther's lead:

- The **1611 King James Bible** still included the Deuterocanonical books in a separate "Apocrypha" section between the Old and New Testaments.

- By the **1800s**, due to cost-cutting measures, growing anti-Catholic sentiment, and Protestant theological bias, the Deuterocanon was **entirely removed** from most Protestant Bibles.

Thus, the Protestant Bible today is **missing seven full books and parts of others** that had been accepted and used by all Christians for over a millennium.

Martin Luther "Edited" the Bible to Match His Opinion

"Ye shall not add unto the word which I command you, neither shall ye diminish ought from it, that ye may keep the commandments of the Lord your God which I command you" (Deut. 4:2).

In Romans 3:28, St. Paul writes, *"For we hold that a person is justified by faith apart from works prescribed by the law."*

Martin Luther, however, inserted the word *"alone"* into his German translation, rendering it: *"faith **alone** apart from works."*

He justified this addition by claiming it clarified Paul's meaning. But this wasn't translation—it was **his preferred interpretation**. The original Greek does **not** contain the word "alone." Luther *added* it to support his novel doctrine of ***sola fide*** (faith alone), which the Church had **never taught** in isolation from grace or works of love (cf. James 2:24, Galatians 5:6).

Luther even admitted in his writings that he added "alone" and didn't care if others objected, saying: *"If your papist makes such an unnecessary row about the word sola, say right out to him: 'Dr. Martin Luther will have it so.'"* (*An Open Letter on Translating*, 1530)

This move shows Luther was not simply trying to recover lost truth but was reshaping Scripture to fit his theology—something no individual has the authority to do.

Protestants Had No Authority to Change the Canon

The authority to determine the canon of Scripture lies with the **Church that Jesus founded**, which Paul calls the "**pillar and foundation of truth**" (1 Timothy 3:15). That Church—**the Catholic Church**—gathered, protected, and proclaimed the Bible.

No individual, not even a Reformer, has the right to override the Church's discernment on what is or isn't the Word of God. When Protestants removed books or altered texts to fit new doctrines, they stepped outside the authority of the very Church that gave them the Bible in the first place. It's ironic they accuse Catholics of following man-made traditions.

To put it plainly: **the Reformers didn't reform Scripture—they edited it according to their own will and by no authority but their own.**

But how can we know the books in the full (original) canon of Scripture are the Bible fully inspired by the Holy Spirit? Let's use reason based on the following facts:

- Out of **approximately 350 Old Testament quotations** in the New Testament, over **300 match the Septuagint**, not the Hebrew text the Protestants kept.

- If Jesus and the Apostles accepted the Septuagint **with the Deuterocanon,** then we must too. Why would Christ Himself refer to a book that is uninspired?

Deuterocanonical Books Quoted or Alluded to by Jesus and the Apostles:

Deuterocanonical Book	Quoted/Alluded	NT Reference	Description
Wisdom of Solomon 2:12–20	Jesus' Passion Narrative (Gospels)	*Matthew 27:41–43*	The mocking of the "righteous man" matches Wisdom's prophecy.
Sirach (Ecclesiasticus) 5:11	James	*James 1:19*	"Be swift to hear, slow to speak" — nearly identical advice.
Sirach 28:2	Jesus	*Matthew 6:14*	Jesus' teaching on forgiving others to be forgiven mirrors Sirach.
Tobit 4:7–11	Jesus	*Luke 14:13–14*	Teaching about almsgiving and heavenly reward echoes Tobit's instructions.
2 Maccabees 6–7	Author of Hebrews	*Hebrews 11:35*	Cites the martyrs who endured torture, hoping in resurrection (story directly from 2 Maccabees).
Baruch 3:36–38	John	*John 1:14*	Baruch speaks of God appearing on earth, matching the Incarnation theme.
Judith 13:18	Elizabeth (Gospel of Luke)	*Luke 1:42*	Elizabeth's praise of Mary ("Blessed are you among women") closely mirrors Judith's praise after victory over evil.

Key Takeaways:

- **Direct matches**: Wisdom → Passion, Sirach → James, Sirach → Sermon on the Mount, Tobit → Jesus' teachings.

- **Allusions and fulfillments**: 2 Maccabees in Hebrews, Baruch in John's Gospel, Judith mirrored by Elizabeth.

- **The Septuagint (LXX)** was the Old Testament **most quoted by Jesus** and the Apostles—and the LXX *included* all the Deuterocanonical books.

- **Jesus Himself** references themes from **Sirach** and **Tobit**.

- **James and Hebrews** explicitly mirror **Sirach** and **2 Maccabees**.

- **Elizabeth's praise** in Luke heavily alludes to language used in **Judith**.

- **Baruch's prophecy** lays the groundwork for the New Testament view of Christ's Incarnation.

Jesus and His Apostles quoted and fulfilled the Deuterocanonical books, treating them as Scripture. They used the Septuagint (LXX), which included these books, **confirming their inspiration** and place in the Christian Bible. The Deuterocanonical books had been recognized and used as Scripture for **about 1,100 to 1,400 years** *before the Protestant Reformation*:

Date	Event	Relevance to the Deuterocanon
1st century AD	Jesus and the Apostles quote from the Septuagint—which contained the Deuterocanon.	The early Church accepted these books as inspired Scripture.
2nd–3rd century BC	The **Septuagint** (Greek Old Testament) was compiled, including the Deuterocanonical books.	Jesus and the Apostles used this version.
Late 4th century AD (382 AD)	The **Council of Rome** (under Pope Damasus I) listed the full canon of Scripture—including the Deuterocanonical books.	First official canon listing for the Church.
393 and 397 AD	**Councils of Hippo and Carthage** reaffirmed the canon, including the Deuterocanon.	These councils guided the entire Western Church.
405 AD	**St. Jerome** completed the **Latin Vulgate** Bible, including the Deuterocanonical books (even though Jerome personally had hesitations, he submitted to Church authority).	The standard Bible of Christendom for 1,000+ years.
1442 AD	The **Council of Florence** formally reaffirmed the canon again, including the Deuterocanon.	Still centuries before the Reformation.
1520s–1530s	**Protestant Reformers** (like Martin Luther) **removed** the Deuterocanon from the Bible, calling them "Apocrypha."	This was a radical and novel break from Christian tradition.

By altering the Bible—removing books that had been recognized and used by early Christians, including Jesus and the Apostles themselves for over a thousand years—the **Reformers introduced confusion and division** into Christianity. Once man set himself as the final authority over Scripture, rather than submitting to the Church Christ established, **endless interpretations and disputes inevitably followed**. Today, the thousands of Protestant denominations are the fruit of that rebellion, each claiming the Bible as their guide yet **disagreeing** on fundamental doctrines. The Reformation was a failure from the start because it placed man's interpretation over God's Church, shattering the visible unity that Christ prayed for (John 17:21) and leaving behind chaos and division where there was once **one faith, one baptism, and one Church** (Ephesians 4:4–5).

Debunking Protestant Objections to the Full Canon

The 400 Years of Silence

Protestants often claim there was a "400-year gap of silence" between the Old and New Testaments, a period where, supposedly, no inspired Scripture was written, and God ceased speaking to His people until the coming of Christ. **This idea is used to justify rejecting the Deuterocanonical books**, which were written during that time. However, the claim **collapses** under historical and biblical scrutiny. The "400 years of silence" is not a biblical teaching. **It is a human invention**, designed after the fact to justify rejecting parts of Scripture that contradict Protestant theology. **There was no silence**. God continued speaking, preparing, and working through His people—and the Deuterocanonical books are part of that story until Jesus came on the scene.

Scripture itself never teaches that God went silent for 400 years. There is no biblical text—Old or New Testament—that says prophecy or divine revelation ceased after Malachi. In fact, the **historical record shows the exact opposite**: during this so-called silent period, faithful Jews believed God was still actively working among them, and significant religious events occurred that prepared the way for Christ. Books like 1 and 2 Maccabees record profound miracles, martyrdoms for the faith, and even angelic interventions—**all consistent** with God's ongoing action in history.

The Council of Jamnia

One of the most common Protestant arguments against the Deuterocanonical books is the claim **that the Jews rejected these books at the "Council of Jamnia" around 90 AD.** However, modern scholarship, including the work of Dr. Brant Pitre, has shown that there is **no evidence** that a formal council ever took place at Jamnia. What did occur was likely an informal gathering of Jewish rabbis discussing various issues of Jewish identity and scripture after the destruction of the Temple—not an official, binding decision on the canon of Scripture. Even if Jamnia had closed a Jewish canon, Christians would not be bound by it. **The same Jewish leaders who would have rejected the Deuterocanon also rejected Jesus as the Messiah and the entire New Testament.** It is the apostolic tradition of the Church, not post-Resurrection rabbinic decisions, that determines the Christian canon.

Errors In the Original Canon

Another objection is that the Deuterocanonical books supposedly contain historical or theological "errors." Protestants argue that these errors disqualify them from being Scripture. However, what they identify as "errors" are often **misunderstandings or exaggerated claims.** Moreover, the books that Protestants accept—such as 1 and 2 Kings and Chronicles—also contain apparent discrepancies when judged by rigid modern standards. The Church has always understood that **Scripture must be read within a living tradition** and not subjected to modern critical standards **divorced from faith.**

Some Protestants claim that Jesus never quoted directly from the Deuterocanonical books and therefore they cannot be inspired. However, Jesus also never directly quoted from several Old Testament books that Protestants retain, such as Esther, Ecclesiastes, Ezra, Nehemiah, and the Song of Songs. If the absence of quotation were the standard for inspiration, Protestants would need to remove these books as well. Clearly, direct quotation is not, and has never been, the standard for inclusion in the canon.

Another point often raised is that some early Church Fathers, most notably St. Jerome, expressed doubts about the Deuterocanonical books. While it is true that Jerome initially preferred the Hebrew texts, **he ultimately submitted to the authority of the Church** and included the Deuterocanonical books in the Latin Vulgate. More importantly, the canon was officially recognized at the Councils of Rome (382 AD), Hippo (393 AD), and Carthage (397 AD), **centuries before the Protestant Reformation**. It was reaffirmed at the Council of Florence (1442 AD) and solemnly defined at the Council of Trent (1546 AD). The Protestant Reformers did not "recover" an original canon; they **rejected the one that had been affirmed by the Church for over a millennium.**

Finally, some Protestants admit that the Deuterocanonical books support Catholic doctrines such as prayers for the dead, purgatory, and the intercession of saints, and for this reason, they reject them. **This objection exposes the true motive behind the Deuterocanon's removal: not historical fidelity but theological convenience. Because these books support doctrines that the Reformers had already decided to reject, they simply discarded the evidence.** This is not a recovery of authentic Christianity but an act of rebellion—an elevation of human opinion over the authority of the Church Christ Himself established. The fruit of that rebellion is evident today in the thousands of Protestant denominations, each claiming to follow Scripture alone yet unable to agree on what Scripture even teaches.

So, as we see again, the Reformation did not restore Christian unity; **it shattered it**—because whenever man places himself above the Church Christ founded, confusion, division, and error are the inevitable results.

"God is not a God of confusion but of peace" (1 Corinthians 14:33)

Conclusion: The Bible Is a Catholic Book Authored by the Holy Spirit

The Catholic Church preserved and transmitted both the Old and New Testaments, carefully discerning which writings were truly inspired by the Holy Spirit. It was the Church—**guided by apostolic tradition and the Magisterium**—that determined the canon of Scripture. Without the Catholic Church, there would be no Bible as we know it today.

One of the most persistent myths among Protestants is the idea that the Catholic Church tried to keep the Bible away from the people. In reality, **the Church sought to protect the Bible**—not from the faithful, but from mistranslation, distortion, and doctrinal abuse. Before the invention of the printing press, Bibles were painstakingly hand-copied by monks, often over the course of years. This made them rare and costly treasures. Most people during the Middle Ages were illiterate, and even if they owned a Bible, they wouldn't have been able to read it. That's why churches were adorned with sacred art, stained glass, and statues—visual catechism that told the story of salvation to rich and poor alike.

The removal of the Deuterocanonical books was not a recovery of lost truth, but a mutilation of Scripture based on human preference. These books had been accepted by Christ, His apostles, and the early Church for over a thousand years. Claims that they were rejected at the so-called Council of Jamnia, or that they contain errors, collapse under **honest historical scrutiny**. The real reason they were discarded is simple: they supported Catholic doctrines the Reformers had already decided to reject. Instead of conforming their theology to Scripture, they conformed Scripture to their theology, setting a **dangerous precedent that continues to fragment Christianity to this day**.

Only the Catholic Church has preserved the full deposit of faith, maintained apostolic succession, and protected the canon of Scripture given by Christ to His Church. It is not built on shifting human opinions but on the solid rock of Peter's confession and Christ's promise that the gates of hell would not prevail against it (Matthew 16:18). **In a world of endless division and confusion, the Catholic Church remains the One, Holy, Catholic, and Apostolic Church** that Christ established—unchanging, authoritative, and guided by the Holy Spirit into all truth.

When certain groups began spreading unauthorized or heretical translations, the Church's response wasn't suppression for power's sake, **but a pastoral duty to preserve the integrity of God's Word. The Church had to ensure that Scripture was not twisted to support false doctrines or manipulated by personal agendas.** Far from hiding the Bible, the Catholic Church protected it, preserved it, translated it, and—guided by the Holy Spirit—defined what belonged in it.

The truth is simple but powerful: the Catholic Church didn't fear the Bible. She cherished it, guarded it, and gave it to the world. For a deeper look at this often-misunderstood history, I recommend Jimmy Akin's excellent book *The Bible Is a Catholic Book*.

What is Worship?
The Sacrificial Pattern in Scripture

For many modern Christians, that word conjures images of emotional music, dynamic preaching, and a well-produced Sunday service. Lights dimmed, hands raised, hearts stirred. These expressions may be sincere, but are they what Scripture means when it speaks of worship? **The Bible tells a different story.** From Genesis to Revelation, **worship has always involved sacrifice.** It is not primarily about how we *feel* but about what we *offer*. This chapter will explore the biblical meaning of worship, the power of the Eucharist, and why Catholic worship is not about the lights or the music—but about the Lamb.

Worship Is About Sacrifice, Not Entertainment

The Hebrew word for worship, *avodah*, literally means work, service, or offering.

In the Bible, **worship has always involved sacrifice.** From the beginning:

- **Abel** offered the best of his flock (Genesis 4:4).

- **Noah** built an altar and offered burnt offerings (Genesis 8:20).

- **Abraham** was willing to sacrifice Isaac (Genesis 22).

- **Moses** and the Israelites offered animal sacrifices in the Temple.

This understanding doesn't disappear in the New Testament—it is fulfilled. In the New Testament, **true worship remains sacrificial**:

"Offer your bodies as a living sacrifice, holy and pleasing to God—this is your spiritual worship" (Romans 12:1).

True worship costs something. It is not passive. It is not a performance. It is participation.

So worship is not:

- A concert.

- A motivational speech.

- A feel-good gathering.

- A Bible study.

Worship is:

- Sacrifice.

- Offering.

- Participation in the death and Resurrection of Jesus.

- Participation in the Supper of the Lamb–The Eucharist.

At the center of Catholic worship is the Mass—the one perfect sacrifice of Christ, made present again on the altar. Just as the Israelites were commanded not only to sacrifice the Passover Lamb but to eat it, we too are called to partake of the true Lamb of God in the Eucharist. The Mass is not a reenactment, not a symbol, not a show. It is a real encounter with Calvary. To worship as Catholics is to step into the heart of salvation history, to stand at the foot of the Cross, and to unite our lives to Christ's eternal offering.

Jesus Is Our Passover Lamb

To understand the Mass, we need to understand the Passover.

In Exodus 12, the Israelites were saved from death by:

1. Sacrificing a spotless lamb.

2. Spreading its blood on their doorposts.

3. Eating the lamb.

If they didn't eat the lamb, the sacrifice was incomplete.

Jesus fulfills this perfectly:

"Behold the Lamb of God who takes away the sins of the world" (John 1:29).

At the Last Supper, Jesus says:

"This is my body... This is my blood... Do this in remembrance of Me" (Luke 22:19).

He becomes the true Passover Lamb:

- Sacrificed on the Cross.

- Blood poured out for our salvation.

- Given to us to consume in the Eucharist.

That's why Catholics go to Mass—not for music or preaching, but to be present at the one perfect sacrifice made present again on the altar.

The Mass Is the Perfect Worship

The Catholic Mass is not a concert or performance—it is a real participation in Christ's once-for-all sacrifice on Calvary (Hebrews 9:23–28).

The Eucharist is:

- The fulfillment of Passover.

- The New Covenant in His blood.

- The worship of heaven itself (see Revelation 5 and 7).

We are not spectators. We are offering ourselves with Christ as a living sacrifice.

This is why Catholics kneel, fast, pray, and approach the altar with reverence—not as consumers of a show, but as worshippers at the foot of the Cross.

Music in Worship: Important, But Not the Main Thing

Music is a beautiful part of Catholic worship—but it supports the sacrifice, it doesn't define it.

- Sacred music is meant to lift the heart to God, not entertain.

- Gregorian chant and hymns developed to honor the mystery of the Eucharist, not mimic pop concerts.

- Modern music can be fine if it's reverent and Christ-centered—but worship is not about the band or the beat.

If the music stops, the sacrifice remains. The power of the Mass is in Christ's presence and sacrifice, not the playlist.

Worship Is About the Lamb, Not the Lights

- Today, many are drawn to churches with hype, lights, and emotional music, but they often leave **spiritually undernourished** because what they experienced was performance, not sacrifice.

  - "We have an altar from which those who serve the tabernacle have no right to eat" (Hebrews 13:10).

- That altar is the Catholic Mass, where Jesus, our Passover Lamb, is offered and received.

- Worship isn't about how we feel.

- It's about what Christ did—and our humble participation in it.

Conclusion: Why We Must Worship Like the Early Church

Worship, in its true biblical sense, is not primarily about music, emotions, or a sermon—it is about offering sacrifice to God. From the Old Testament to the New, worship always involved a priest, an altar, and a sacrifice. **In the New Covenant, Jesus is the Eternal High Priest who offers Himself as the once-for-all sacrifice on the Cross, and this sacrifice is made present at every Catholic Mass.**

The Mass is the authentic act of Christian worship because it is not just a remembrance—it is a real participation in the sacrifice of Christ, as He commanded at the Last Supper: "Do this in remembrance of Me." Protestant services, while often sincere, focus mainly on preaching and praise but lack **the Eucharistic sacrifice, the very heart of Christian worship**. Only the Mass unites the Church with Christ's sacrifice on Calvary, which is why it is the true and full expression of Christian worship.

The Seven Sacraments:
God's Visible Grace

From the very beginning, Christianity has never been merely a set of beliefs or moral principles. It is a lived encounter with the living God—one that engages our minds, our hearts, and our bodies. In Catholicism, this encounter happens most powerfully through the **seven sacraments**: Baptism, Confirmation, the Eucharist, Confession (also called Reconciliation), Anointing of the Sick, Marriage, and Holy Orders. These are not empty rituals or mere symbols. They are **real, physical means by which God communicates His grace**—acts of divine power that affect what they signify. In a world obsessed with the material and often blind to the spiritual, the sacraments are where the invisible breaks into the visible—where heaven touches earth.

The Catechism of the Catholic Church teaches that sacraments are "efficacious signs of grace, instituted by Christ and entrusted to the Church, by which divine life is dispensed to us" (CCC 1131). In other words, they don't just point to something spiritual; they **actually do something**. Like medicine for the soul, they are supernatural remedies for our fallen condition and sustaining nourishment for our journey home.

Sign vs. Symbol: What's the Difference?

In everyday language, we often use the words **sign** and **symbol** interchangeably. But in Catholic theology—especially when discussing the sacraments—they mean very different things.

A symbol points to something else but doesn't actually do or contain it.

- It **represents** a reality, but it **doesn't participate in it.**

- Example: A **wedding ring** is a symbol of marriage. It represents the bond between spouses, but it isn't the bond itself.

- In Protestant theology, baptism or communion is often seen this way: as a **symbol of inner faith**—important, but not transformative in itself.

A sign, especially in the sacramental sense, does more than represent—it reveals and makes present the spiritual reality it signifies.

- A sacrament is a **visible sign of an invisible grace** (CCC 1131).

- It not only **points to a spiritual truth**, but **actually causes** that grace to take effect in the soul.

Think of it like this:

- A symbol = a reminder.

- A sign = a real encounter.

In Catholic sacramental theology, **a sign is not just outward theater**. It is the physical expression of something **real and active** taking place at the spiritual level. It's not a metaphor—it's a mechanism. The sacraments aren't symbolic gestures. They are **real signs** instituted by Christ that **confer the grace they signify**. God uses matter—water, oil, bread, wine—as channels of divine power. Through the sacraments, heaven and earth collide and something truly happens, both visibly and invisibly.

Let's begin with a brief overview of each sacrament, followed by a deeper exploration of what makes them not only biblical and historical, but **essential** for the Christian life.

The Seven Sacraments:

1. **Baptism** – The sacrament of spiritual rebirth; through it we are cleansed of original sin and become members of Christ's Body, the Church.

2. **Confirmation** – The strengthening of baptismal grace; we are sealed with the Holy Spirit and empowered to live out our faith boldly.

3. **The Eucharist** – The source and summit of Christian life; we receive Jesus Himself—Body, Blood, Soul, and Divinity—under the appearance of bread and wine.

4. **Reconciliation (Confession)** – The sacrament of healing and forgiveness; we are restored to grace and reconciled with God and the Church.

5. **Anointing of the Sick** – A sacrament of spiritual (and sometimes physical) healing for those facing serious illness, suffering, or death.

6. **Holy Matrimony (Marriage)** – A covenant of life and love between a man and woman, which reflects the union between Christ and His Church.

7. **Holy Orders** – The sacrament through which men are ordained for service in the priesthood, becoming instruments of Christ's presence in the Church.

Baptism

Baptism is the gateway to all the other sacraments. Through water and the Spirit, we are cleansed of **original sin** and become adopted children of God. **Jesus Himself was baptized (Matthew 3:13–17), not because He needed cleansing, but to consecrate the waters for us.** The early

Church Fathers often taught that Christ didn't become holy by the waters—the waters became holy by Christ. St. Gregory of Nazianzus wrote, "He comes to sanctify the Jordan for our sake... He comes to bury the old Adam in the water."

In submitting to baptism, Jesus didn't merely set an example. He inaugurated a new creation. Heaven was opened, the Spirit descended, and the Father spoke—revealing the divine reality baptism participates in. **Far from being a mere symbol, baptism is where Christ begins His mission and where we begin ours.**

Scripture does not describe baptism as a ritual bath or symbolic gesture. In 1 Peter 3:21, the apostle states directly: "Baptism now saves you—not as a removal of dirt from the body but as an appeal to God for a good conscience, through the resurrection of Jesus Christ." The Greek word for "appeal" (eperōtēma) also means *pledge* or *response*, emphasizing the spiritual transaction taking place. Peter compares baptism to the waters that saved Noah and his family. If baptism is just a metaphor, then bathtubs would have salvific power—which is absurd.

Titus 3:5 is just as clear: "He saved us... by the washing of *regeneration and renewal* of the Holy Spirit." The Greek phrase here—loutron palingenesias—literally means a "washing of rebirth." It was a technical term used by the early Church to describe the sacrament of baptism. This fits perfectly with John 3:5: "Unless one is born of water and Spirit, he cannot enter the kingdom of God." **Rebirth is not metaphorical; it's sacramental. God works through the visible to bring about the invisible.**

Acts 22:16 further confirms this: "Rise and be baptized and wash away your sins, calling on His name." And Romans 6:4 declares, "We were buried therefore with him by baptism into death, so that... we too might walk in newness of life." Baptism unites us with Christ's death and resurrection in a real, grace-giving way.

Additionally, baptism fulfills and surpasses the Old Covenant sign of circumcision. In the Old Testament, circumcision was the **visible sign** of entering God's covenant—performed on infants as a means of belonging to God's family (Genesis 17:10–14). In the New Covenant, St. Paul reveals in Colossians 2:11–12 that baptism now serves this role: "In Him you were also circumcised… having been buried with Him in baptism." Just as circumcision marked one as part of God's people, baptism does the same—but with spiritual regeneration.

The early Christians didn't invent these ideas. They received them from Christ and the apostles. For 1500 years, no Christian questioned the salvific power of baptism. It was only with the Reformation that some began preaching otherwise—disconnected from both Scripture and the universal witness of the early Church.

To be baptized is to be born again. Not symbolically—but sacramentally. Through water and the Spirit, God gives us new life.

Confirmation

Confirmation is one of the most underrated sacraments in the Catholic Church. Some see it as a sort of "Catholic graduation ceremony," where teenagers show up with cringey robes, memorize a few answers, and check the sacramental box before disappearing from Mass for the next 10 years. But that's not the Church's vision—and certainly not the biblical one.

Confirmation is not a rite of passage. It's a rite of power.

It's the moment when God **seals** us with His Holy Spirit, **strengthens** what began in baptism, and **commissions** us to live boldly as soldiers of Christ.

Biblical Foundations: Sealed with the Spirit

The idea of being sealed by the Holy Spirit didn't come from a Vatican committee—it came from the New Testament:

- In **Acts 8:14–17**, the apostles in Jerusalem hear that Samaritans have "accepted the word of God" and been baptized. But something's missing. So Peter and John go down and **lay hands on them**, and *then* they receive the Holy Spirit. Baptism gave new birth; **confirmation gave power.**

- In **Acts 19:5–6**, Paul meets believers who were baptized but hadn't received the Holy Spirit. After clarifying their baptism, he lays hands on them, and "the Holy Spirit came upon them," manifesting in boldness and prophecy.

- St. Paul writes in **Ephesians 1:13**, "You were sealed with the promised Holy Spirit." That language—**"sealed"**—is sacramental. You're not just spiritually inspired. You're marked.

This isn't a Pentecostal adrenaline rush. It's a sacramental empowerment.

Old Testament Typology: Anointed for Mission

Throughout salvation history, when God appointed someone to a special role—**king, priest, or prophet**—He didn't just give them advice. He **anointed them with oil**, symbolizing the Holy Spirit coming upon them for a specific mission.

- **David** was anointed by Samuel, and "the Spirit of the Lord rushed upon him" (1 Samuel 16:13).

- The **priests of Aaron's line** were anointed and consecrated to serve in God's presence (Exodus 29:7).

- **Elisha** received the prophetic mantle from Elijah, along with a double portion of the Spirit (2 Kings 2:9–15).

In the New Covenant, **Confirmation** is our anointing. We are sealed with sacred chrism by the bishop (a direct successor of the apostles), just as the apostles laid hands on believers in Acts. We're not anointed to rule a kingdom of this world, but to serve the Kingdom of Heaven.

Some Protestants will ask, "If I already have the Holy Spirit, why do I need Confirmation?"

Great question.

First, let's clear this up: **Confirmation doesn't mean you didn't receive the Spirit at baptism. You did.** But Scripture shows us **a deepening, a strengthening, a commissioning** that comes through the laying on of hands—a second grace, not a redundant one.

Think of it like this: Baptism gives you **spiritual life**. Confirmation gives you **spiritual muscle**.

You've been born again—now it's time to stand up, speak out, and fight the good fight.

And logically, if we believe God works through men to **preach**, **heal**, **baptize**, and **marry**, why would we suddenly reject the idea that He can work through the Church to confirm and empower?

- **St. Cyril of Jerusalem (c. 350 A.D.):**

  "Just as Christ, after His baptism and the coming of the Holy Spirit, went forth to do mighty works... so you also, after Holy Baptism and the Mystical Chrism, are made sharers in Christ."

- **St. Ambrose (c. 390 A.D.):**

  "Remember that you received the spiritual seal, the Spirit of wisdom and understanding... the Spirit of knowledge and reverence, the Spirit of holy fear."

- **The Apostolic Tradition (c. 215 A.D., attributed to Hippolytus)** describes bishops anointing and laying hands on the baptized, invoking the Spirit: "Pour out upon them your Holy Spirit, the Spirit of grace... and strengthen them in your fear."

This wasn't a later invention—it was **apostolic continuity**. Always tied to the laying on of hands. Always for strengthening the baptized in faith and mission. In a culture that reduces faith to feelings and sacraments to symbolism, Confirmation reminds us that Christianity is not passive. It's not just a worldview—it's warfare. And God doesn't send His people to battle unarmed.

Confirmation is not about emotional maturity. It's about spiritual readiness. You were baptized into Christ. In Confirmation, you are **anointed for battle**. You're not just invited to believe. You're commissioned to **witness**.

The Eucharist

Of all the sacraments, the **Eucharist** is the most misunderstood—and the most attacked. Many today say it's just a symbol, a memorial, or a nice church tradition. But Scripture, history, and 2,000 years of Christian witness say otherwise. The Eucharist isn't just **like** Jesus. It **is** Jesus—Body, Blood, Soul, and Divinity—offered under the appearance of bread and wine. That's not symbolic rhetoric. That's real theology. **And it's been the belief of the Church from the very beginning.**

Let's start with the biblical blueprint. God didn't drop the Eucharist on us out of nowhere. He prepared us for it from Genesis to the Gospels:

- In **Exodus**, the Israelites were saved through the blood of the **Passover Lamb**, which had to be eaten. Jesus is the true Lamb of God (John 1:29), and at the Last Supper, He didn't say, "This represents My Body." He said, "This **is** My Body... This **is** My Blood" (Luke 22:19–20).

- In the desert, God fed His people with **manna from Heaven**—miraculous bread that sustained them physically. Jesus says in John 6: "I am the living bread that came down from Heaven… and the bread that I will give is My flesh for the life of the world" (John 6:51).

- In the Tabernacle, the priests kept the **Bread of the Presence**, a mysterious holy bread that prefigured the Real Presence of Christ in the Eucharist.

- And let's not forget **Melchizedek**, the king and priest who offered bread and wine to Abraham (Genesis 14:18). He's a "type" of Christ, our eternal High Priest, who does the very same in the Mass.

Now flip to the New Testament:

We'll cover the Eucharist in more depth in a later chapter, but in **John 6**, Jesus tells His disciples—repeatedly—that His flesh is real food and His blood is real drink.

"Unless you eat the flesh of the Son of Man and drink His blood, you have no life in you" (John 6:53).

That's either true—or it's heresy. There's no middle ground.

And then we have **1 Corinthians 11**, where St. Paul warns believers not to receive the Eucharist **unworthily**, because they would be "**guilty of profaning the Body and Blood of the Lord**" (v. 27). If it's just a symbol, how could you be guilty of profaning the actual Body and Blood? You can't desecrate a metaphor.

Even after the Resurrection, Jesus is still making His Real Presence known in the breaking of the bread. In Luke 24, the disciples on the road to Emmaus don't recognize Him—until He breaks bread. Then their eyes are opened. Sound familiar?

And the early Church Fathers were crystal clear:

- **St. Ignatius of Antioch (c. 107 A.D.):**

  "They abstain from the Eucharist because they do not confess that the Eucharist is the flesh of our Savior Jesus Christ..."

- **St. Justin Martyr (c. 150 A.D.):**

  "We do not receive these as common bread or common drink... the food which has been made into the Eucharist... is both the flesh and blood of that incarnated Jesus."

- **St. Irenaeus (c. 180 A.D.):**

  "The bread... becomes the Eucharist of the Body of Christ, and the wine the Blood."

This wasn't later Catholic dogma. It was the **unanimous voice** of the early Church. No one dies for a metaphor. **The early Christians risked their lives for the Mass.** The Eucharist was the **center** of Christian worship from the very beginning—not a side dish. As Flannery O'Connor once said, "If it's just a symbol, to hell with it."

The Eucharist isn't a nice reminder. It's a **participation** in the once-for-all sacrifice of Christ made present on the altar, outside of time. It's Heaven on earth. It's food for the journey.

Reconciliation (Confession)

One of the most misunderstood—and yet most beautiful—sacraments in the Catholic Church is **Confession** (also called Reconciliation or Penance). Protestants often ask, *"Why confess your sins to a priest when you can just go straight to God?"* And at first glance, it sounds like a fair question. But let's look deeper—biblically, historically, and even logically.

Confession in the Old Covenant

God has always used **priests** as **mediators of mercy**. In Leviticus 5:5–6, when someone sinned, they were required to **confess** their sin and then bring a guilt offering to the priest, who would make atonement for them. The priest was not just a bystander—he was part of the process God established for forgiveness. Leviticus 19:21–22 reaffirms this pattern:

"The priest shall make atonement for him… and he shall be forgiven."

This wasn't because God *couldn't* forgive directly. It was because He chose to work **through** the priesthood. Why? Because sin damages both our relationship with God and our standing in the community. The priest acted as a **visible sign of reconciliation** with both.

So when someone claims confession to a priest is "man-made," we can kindly ask: *Have you read Leviticus?*

The New Covenant Fulfillment

Jesus didn't eliminate the priesthood—He fulfilled it. And what was the first thing the Risen Christ did when He appeared to the apostles?

"He breathed on them and said, 'Receive the Holy Spirit. If you forgive the sins of any, they are forgiven them; if you retain the sins of any, they are retained'" (John 20:22–23).

He didn't say, *"Tell people to confess directly to Me."* He **delegated authority**—divine authority—to His apostles to **forgive sins**. That power wasn't symbolic. You don't symbolically retain sins. Jesus gave them His own authority to reconcile sinners with God—something He had been doing visibly for three years. This was not optional. It was **sacramental**.

But Can't I Just Go Straight to Jesus?

Let's be honest—this is the Protestant default: *"Why do I need a priest when I have Jesus?"* It sounds pious. But let's test the logic:

- If we can "just go straight to Jesus" for everything, then...

  - Why do we have **pastors**?

  - Why do we call **911** instead of just praying for healing?

  - Why do Pentecostals lay hands on each other for healing?

  - Why do we ask people to pray for us at all?

If God never uses human instruments, then marriage, parenting, and spiritual leadership should be pointless. But they're not. **Scripture is clear that God uses people**—*flawed, human people*—to mediate His grace, authority, healing, and guidance. *"Confess your sins to one another..."* (James 5:16). Why does James say this if we can always "just go straight to God"?

Confession Isn't About the Priest

It's About God's Power. **The priest is not the source of forgiveness**. Christ is. But Jesus gave His authority to the apostles and their successors to act in His name. When a priest absolves you, he says: *"I absolve you from your sins..."* Why? Because that's exactly what Jesus empowered him to do (John 20:23).

And to be clear, this isn't about a priest "knowing your secrets." He's heard it all. In fact, he's **bound by the seal of confession** under penalty of automatic excommunication if he ever reveals what was said. This is **not therapy. It's a spiritual operation.** You don't go to confession to feel better. You go to **be forgiven.** The Early Church Fathers agree:

- **St. Cyprian of Carthage (250 A.D.):**

  "Do you think that you still stand fast, when you withdraw from the bishops and the clergy? ... If he who confesses his sin does penance with his whole heart, the satisfaction of the priest will obtain from the Lord."

- **St. Basil the Great (370 A.D.):**

  "It is necessary to confess our sins to those to whom the dispensation of God's mysteries is entrusted."

- **St. John Chrysostom (c. 390 A.D.):**

  "Priests have received a power which God has given neither to angels nor to archangels... God above confirms what the priests do here below."

For the first 1500 years of Christianity, **confession to a priest** was the **unquestioned norm**. It was the Protestant Reformers who broke with that tradition—not because of Scripture, but because of new theology.

Sin is not just "between me and God." **It wounds the Body of Christ** (1 Corinthians 12). It requires healing in both vertical and horizontal dimensions. The priest stands as Christ's visible minister, offering reconciliation to both God and the Church. Confession is **not spiritual red tape**. It's **spiritual surgery**. God made us body and soul. Therefore, His forgiveness comes to us both spiritually and **physically**—through real words spoken by a real man acting in the name of Christ.

If we trust God to use **ordinary men** to preach, teach, baptize, anoint, and marry—why draw the line at forgiving sins? He's the same Jesus. Still healing the same way. Still working through His Body, the Church.

Anointing of the Sick

This sacrament is rooted in James 5:14–15, where the sick are anointed with oil and prayed over for healing and forgiveness. It brings spiritual strength, peace, and often physical healing, according to God's will. Anointing unites the sufferer to Christ's Passion, offering redemptive meaning to pain and preparing the soul for eternity if death is near. For many Catholics—and nearly all non-Catholics—Anointing of the Sick is misunderstood as little more than **"last rites"**: something you call for when someone's on their deathbed and it's time to give them a spiritual send-off. But that's a distortion of what this sacrament actually is. Anointing of the Sick is not just for the dying—it's for the **suffering**. It's not about defeat; it's about grace in the fight.

God has always cared about healing the whole person—body and soul. In the Old Testament, healing was tied to **sacrifice and intercession**. Priests prayed over the sick and offered atonement for them (Leviticus 14:18–20). Oil was used both medicinally and symbolically: for anointing kings, priests, and prophets, but also for binding wounds (Isaiah 1:6). So when James writes in the New Testament, "Is any among you sick? Let him call for the elders of the Church, and let them pray over him, anointing him with oil in the name of the Lord" (James 5:14–15), he's not pulling this practice out of thin air. He's rooting it in a long tradition of **God working through both the physical and the spiritual to bring healing**.

Praying for the sick is great, but James doesn't say to just, "pray *for* the sick." He says, **"anoint them,"** because that physical act—performed by those in apostolic authority—**conveys real healing grace**.

The early Church took this seriously. St. Hippolytus (third century) mentions the use of blessed oil by bishops for healing. St. Cyril of Alexandria taught that the sacrament brings "health to the soul and forgiveness of sins." And by the 4th century, St. John Chrysostom affirmed that the sacrament had power to heal, restore, and strengthen both body and soul.

The Catechism teaches that Anointing of the Sick unites the suffering with the Passion of Christ, gives peace and courage, forgives sins (if the person is unable to confess), and sometimes—by God's will—**restores physical health** (CCC 1520–1523). It's not magic, but it's not symbolic either. It is a **real, grace-filled encounter with the healing Christ**, especially in moments when we are weakest.

This is the God who touches lepers. Who spits on dirt to heal blindness. Who raises the dead with a word. He didn't shy away from physical suffering—and He didn't limit healing to metaphor.

So why do we think the sacrament of the sick is just a symbolic comfort? Why do we reduce it to a farewell ritual when Scripture says it's a **channel of forgiveness and restoration**?

Anointing of the Sick is **not the Catholic version of hospice**. It's Jesus meeting you in the pain, in the hospital room, in the moment of crisis. It's the sacrament of **hope**, not despair. It's a declaration that God is still with you—even here, even now—and that suffering never has the final word.

Holy Matrimony (Marriage)

Marriage is not merely a legal contract. It is a covenant mirroring the relationship between Christ and His Church (Ephesians 5:25–32). In Matrimony, the couple become living icons of divine love. Grace is given not only to love, but to persevere, sacrifice, and raise a family in faith. The love between spouses becomes a channel of God's love. Marriage is not a human invention. It's not a social construct. It's not just a romantic partnership or a legal agreement. **Marriage is a sacrament—a sacred covenant instituted by God from the very beginning and elevated by Christ to be a channel of grace.**

In Genesis 2, before there were nations, governments, or even the Ten Commandments, there was a marriage. God creates Eve from Adam's side and brings her to him—not as property, but as a partner. "The two shall become one flesh," Scripture says, and Jesus later quotes this Himself, adding: *"What God has joined together, let no man separate"* (Matthew 19:6). That's not a metaphor. That's theology. And it's rooted in a reality as ancient as Eden itself.

Marriage is a living icon of something bigger. St. Paul calls it a **"great mystery" (Mysterion)** in Ephesians 5—because it points to Christ's relationship with His Church. A faithful, fruitful, permanent, life-giving union. That's why Christian marriage isn't just about two people in love. It's about two people becoming **a sign of divine love**—a visible witness of the invisible reality of God's covenant with humanity.

Throughout Scripture, God reveals His love for His people in marital terms. Israel is the unfaithful bride; God is the relentless husband (see Hosea). In the New Testament, Jesus is the **Bridegroom**, and the Church is the **Bride**. Revelation ends not with a war, but with a **wedding feast**—the marriage supper of the Lamb (Revelation 19:7). That's not coincidence. Earthly marriage points toward heavenly union.

So when two baptized Christians marry, it's not just a ceremony with pretty flowers and personalized vows. It becomes a **sacramental bond**, sealed by grace. And that grace isn't just for the wedding day—it's for a lifetime. Marriage gives supernatural strength to love, to forgive, to serve, to suffer well, **and to stay faithful when the world says to walk away**.

St. Augustine called marriage a "sacrament of the Church." **Tertullian**, in the third century, wrote, "How beautiful, then, the marriage of two Christians… under the hand of the Church." It wasn't treated lightly. It wasn't revocable. It was holy.

That's why the Church teaches that **marriage is indissoluble**—because it's rooted not in human convenience, but in God's covenantal design. Yes, annulments exist, but they are not a "Catholic divorce" they recognize when a **valid sacrament never truly took place to begin with**. They're a safeguard to protect the sanctity of the real thing.

And no, marriage is not just about procreation. But it's not **less** than that either. Marriage is meant to be open to life—not because the Church wants to count heads, but because love, by nature, is **generative**. Rooted from the Latin verb *generare*, meaning **"to beget," "to produce," or "to bring forth,"** this Latin term comes from the older Proto-Indo-European root *gen-*, which means **"to give birth" or "to produce."** It's the same root found in both Latin and Greek terms related to origin, life, and creation. Take a look at the connections here:

- **Genesis** – from the Greek *genesis* (γένεσις), meaning *origin, creation, or beginning*. The first book of the Bible is literally about the **beginning of life** and creation.

- **Generation** – from Latin *generatio*, meaning the act of begetting or producing (generating) offspring.

- **Generative** – describes something with the **power to produce or reproduce**, especially in terms of life or creativity.

- **Gender** – originally from Latin *genus*, meaning "kind" or "type," but related to *generare*, because it referred to **biological kinds**—male and female—as reproductive categories.

- **Genitals** – from Latin *genitalia*, literally meaning "organs of generation," as they are the **instruments of reproduction**.

These aren't disconnected terms. They all reflect the idea of **life-giving capacity**, **origin**, and **creative potential**—which is why Catholic teaching links sexuality and gender to divine purpose, not just identity. In short: **to generate is to reflect the Creator.**

A love that mirrors God's love should be **faithful, total, fruitful, and free**. In a culture that treats marriage like a contract, Catholicism reminds us: this is a **covenant**. In a world that says love is just a feeling, the Church says love is a **sacrificial act of the will**. In a society that says "follow your heart," we say "follow the Cross"—because that's the kind of love that actually saves.

The world may try to redefine marriage, but the blueprint hasn't changed. It was etched into creation, sanctified by Christ, and sustained by grace. Holy Matrimony isn't outdated—it's eternal.

Holy Orders

In Holy Orders, men are configured to Christ as servant leaders in the Church. Jesus chose and ordained His apostles (John 20:21–23), and they in turn ordained others (Acts 14:23, 2 Timothy 2:2). Through ordination, priests and bishops become sacramental instruments through whom Christ teaches, sanctifies, and governs His Church. If Baptism gives us new life, and Confirmation strengthens us for battle, **Holy Orders** is how Christ ensures the Church will have spiritual fathers to feed, lead, and guard His flock until the end of time. It's not a man-made hierarchy—it's a sacrament of divine continuity. And it goes all the way back to the **Old Covenant priesthood**, fulfilled and transformed in the New.

God has always worked through **ordained men** to serve His people. In the Old Testament, the tribe of Levi was set apart for sacred duties. Priests offered sacrifice, taught the Law, declared forgiveness of sins, and acted as mediators between God and His people. None of this was symbolic. It was physical, liturgical, hierarchical—and divinely commanded.

In the New Covenant, Christ does not abolish priesthood—He fulfills and transforms it. He becomes the High Priest (Hebrews 4:14), the once-for-all sacrifice (Hebrews 10:12), and the one Mediator between

God and man (1 Timothy 2:5). But He also **chooses and ordains men to share in that priesthood**—not to replace Him, but to act in His name.

When Jesus breathes on the apostles and says, *"Receive the Holy Spirit. If you forgive the sins of any, they are forgiven"* (John 20:22–23), He is doing more than comforting them. He is **conferring authority**. When He tells them, *"Do this in memory of Me"* (Luke 22:19), He is instituting both the Eucharist and the sacramental priesthood. These aren't vague symbolic gestures. They are commissions. Christ gives His apostles the authority to teach, govern, and sanctify—in short, to **minister in His person**.

And this wasn't a one-time thing. The apostles laid hands on others (Acts 6:6, Acts 13:3, 1 Timothy 4:14), passing on their authority in what we now call **apostolic succession**. From generation to generation, the priesthood has been handed down through **Holy Orders**, connecting today's Catholic priests directly back to the first apostles. That's not metaphorical lineage. It's historical continuity.

St. Ignatius of Antioch, writing in 107 A.D.—a disciple of John the Apostle—warned Christians not to do anything apart from the bishop, calling obedience to the bishop obedience to God. **Tertullian**, **Clement of Rome**, **Hippolytus**, and countless other early Christian voices affirmed the structure of bishops, priests, and deacons ordained to serve and lead the Church—not as a human institution, but as a divine design.

But let's pause and ask the modern question: *Why do we even need priests? Why can't we all just go directly to Jesus?*

The answer: **you can**—but Jesus still chose to give us **men to act in His name**. This isn't new. He always has. He gave Moses. He gave the Levites. He gave prophets, judges, kings, apostles. And today, He gives priests—not to replace Himself, but to represent Him. When a priest offers Mass, baptizes, absolves sins, or anoints the sick, he does so **in persona Christi**—"in the person of Christ." The priest is not the source of grace—he is the vessel. The instrument. The visible sign.

Let's be honest: Protestants don't bat an eye when a pastor preaches, counsels, or lays hands in prayer. Pentecostals believe the Spirit moves through men. Evangelicals receive altar calls from spiritual leaders. So why is it "man-made religion" when Catholics say Jesus works through **ordained** ministers with apostolic succession?

And yet, even beyond their sacramental role, Catholic priests embody a deeper spiritual truth through the very way they live. Priestly celibacy, though a discipline and not a doctrine, flows naturally from the reality of the priest's identity: he is not a bachelor—he is married to Christ and His Church. Just as Christ is the Bridegroom who lays down His life for His Bride, the priest models that same total self-gift. By forgoing earthly marriage, he lives out a radical availability to God and His people, becoming a spiritual father to many rather than a physical father to a few. This isn't a rejection of marriage—it's a sign that points to the heavenly union we're all ultimately made for.

Holy Orders is not spiritual elitism. It's **spiritual fatherhood**. In a culture desperate for authority and starving for father figures, the Catholic Church dares to say: God still raises up men to lead in humility, to offer sacrifice, to hear confessions, to anoint the dying, and to speak the words *"This is My Body"* so Christ Himself becomes present.

Conclusion: The Visible Signs of an Invisible Reality

The sacraments are not optional Catholic addendum or symbolic ceremonies to mark religious milestones. They are **the way Jesus continues to work in the world**—tangible, physical signs that actually do what they signify. They are the very means by which Christ pours His grace into our lives, not because God is limited to sacraments, but because

we are—we are physical, embodied souls who need physical signs to encounter spiritual realities.

From Baptism to Anointing of the Sick, each sacrament is rooted in Scripture, prefigured in the Old Testament, affirmed by the early Church, and still alive in the Church today. They are not empty rituals or human traditions. They are **divine interventions**—God breaking into our reality again and again with mercy, power, and presence.

Every sacrament is a moment of encounter: with the Trinity, with grace, with the living Body of Christ. And each one is an act of obedience— **not to the Church as an institution, but to Jesus**, who said "Do this," "Go and baptize," "Whose sins you forgive," and "Unless you eat…"

You don't need to invent new ways to feel close to God. You don't need to guess or grasp. Christ already gave us the roadmap. The sacraments are how heaven touches earth. They are how Jesus remains with us—not in theory, but in power.

So don't just believe in grace. **Receive it.**

The sacraments are the medicine. The Church is the hospital. And Jesus is still the Great Physician.

Because the Word didn't just become flesh once. Through the sacraments, **He still does**.

The Eucharist in Scripture:
Sacrament Not Symbol

One of the most radical and beautiful claims of the Catholic Church is this: **Jesus Christ is truly present—Body, Blood, Soul, and Divinity—in the Eucharist**. This isn't symbolic language or dramatic imagery. It is the literal teaching of Christ Himself, and it has been the unbroken belief of the Church from the very beginning. In John 6:53–56, Jesus makes it clear: "Unless you eat the flesh of the Son of Man and drink His blood, you have no life in you." Many walked away from Him that day, unable to accept such a hard teaching—but the Church never has.

Transubstantiation

Transubstantiation is the Church's term for the **miraculous change** that occurs at every Catholic Mass **during the consecration of the bread and wine**. Though the outward appearances—what we see, touch, and taste—remain the same, the inner reality (the "substance") is completely changed. **The bread becomes the true Body of Christ, and the wine becomes His true Blood. This is not a symbolic gesture or a spiritualized remembrance**; it is the real, substantial presence of Jesus Christ under the forms of bread and wine. This change happens by the power of Christ's own words ("This is my body... This is my blood") and through the ministry of the priest, who acts *in persona Christi*—in the person of Christ—during the Mass.

When we receive Holy Communion, we are not receiving a dead body, but the living, glorified, resurrected Christ—Body, Blood, Soul, and Divinity. Jesus' humanity and divinity cannot be separated; where His Body is, His Blood, Soul, and Divinity are also fully present. **In the**

Eucharist, we are united to the Risen Christ in the most intimate way possible this side of heaven. His living flesh becomes our spiritual nourishment, strengthening us with divine grace, deepening our union with Him, and helping to transform us into His likeness. Although the Eucharist remains a profound sacred mystery—something we accept in faith—it is a real participation in the heavenly banquet and the eternal life Christ promised to those who eat His flesh and drink His blood (John 6:54).

The Didache

This doctrine, known as the Real Presence, was not a later invention of the medieval Church or a theological upgrade by overzealous popes. **It was believed and practiced from the start.** In fact, some of the earliest Christian writings outside of Scripture confirm it—perhaps most notably in a document called the *Didache* (pronounced DID-uh-kay). Written as early as 70–90 AD, the Didache, or "The Teaching of the Twelve Apostles," offers a glimpse into the liturgical and moral life of the first Christians. Like the modern-day Catechism of the Catholic Church, it outlines practices like baptism, fasting, prayer, and communal worship—and **it places striking emphasis on the reverence due to the Eucharist.**

- **Date**: Around 70–90 AD (scholars believe as early as 50 AD in some parts).

- **Author**: Attributed to the teaching of the apostles.

- **Importance**: It shows us how the early Church functioned practically, just **one generation** after Christ's Ascension.

This short but powerful document reveals a Church already rooted in sacramental worship, **with the Eucharist at its center**. The reverence, the structure, the language of sacrifice all echo the Catholic Mass far more than any modern-day communion service. If we want to understand how the apostles and their immediate successors under-stood Christ's command to "do this in remembrance of me," **we must listen to the voices closest to them**. This chapter will explore the bibli-cal foundation for the Eucharist, the testimony of the early Church, and why the Real Presence remains the beating heart of Catholic life today.

The Didache, while not "an inspired" book of the Bible, is solid evidence that would hold up in court. It confirms that **Christianity was already sacramental, liturgical, and hierarchical**, resembling the Catholic Church and not modern Protestant communities. Visit the Holy Lands and see if you find an ancient Protestant church… you won't.

What Does the Didache Say About the Eucharist?

- The Eucharist Was a Sacred, Structured Liturgy

Chapters 9 and 10 of the Didache provide specific prayers for the Eucharist—called the "Thanksgiving" (from the Greek *eucharistia*). It distinguishes between the bread and the cup, just like the Gospels and St. Paul do.

Didache 9:1-2: "Concerning the Eucharist, give thanks this way. First, concerning the cup: 'We give You thanks, our Father, for the holy vine of David Your servant, which You have made known to us through Jesus Your Servant. To You be the glory forever.'

And concerning the broken bread: 'We give You thanks, our Father, for the life and knowledge which You have made known to us through Jesus Your Servant. To You be the glory forever.'"

These prayers show the liturgical and reverent nature of early Christian worship—not casual or symbolic, but formal and sacred.

- The Eucharist Was Only for the Baptized and Believing

The Didache clearly warns that only baptized, faithful Christians could receive the Eucharist.

Didache 9:5: "Let no one eat or drink of your Eucharist except those who have been baptized into the name of the Lord. For concerning this also the Lord has said, 'Do not give what is holy to dogs.'"

This shows that early Christians believed the Eucharist was not ordinary bread and wine, but something holy and exclusive—just like the Catholic Church teaches today.

- Eucharist as Unity and Fulfillment

Didache 9:4: "As this broken bread was scattered upon the mountains and being gathered together became one, so let Your Church be gathered together from the ends of the earth into Your kingdom."

This reflects the theology that the Eucharist unites the Church, both spiritually and sacramentally—a very Catholic understanding of communion as both vertical (with God) and horizontal (with the Church).

In summary, **The Didache shows clearly that the early Church believed in the Eucharist as a sacred, communal, and exclusive mystery, not merely symbolic.** It confirms that the Eucharist was already liturgical, sacramental, and closely tied to Church authority and baptism—exactly what the Catholic Church teaches today.

The Passover Meal: The Eucharist as the New Passover

The Eucharist is deeply rooted in Jewish tradition and is the fulfillment of various Old Testament typologies and prophecies. Jesus, as the Messiah, instituted the Eucharist within the context of Passover, **transforming it into the new and everlasting covenant.** Here's how the Eucharist is prefigured in Jewish history and fulfilled in Christ:

- In Exodus 12, God commands the Israelites to sacrifice a spotless lamb and eat it to be spared from death.

- The Israelites had to:

    1. **Sacrifice the Lamb** → Jesus is the Lamb of God (John 1:29).

    2. **Eat the Lamb** → Jesus commands us to eat His Body (John 6:53).

    3. **Mark their doors with blood** → Jesus' blood is shed on the Cross for salvation.

At the Last Supper (a Passover meal), Jesus replaces the sacrificial lamb with Himself, saying:

"This is my body... this is my blood... Do this in **remembrance** of Me" (Luke 22:19–20).

The Greek word used for remembrance here is ἀνάμνησις (*anamnesis*).

Modern Western Meaning:

We often think of *remembrance* as a mental act—recalling something that happened in the past. However, let's look at **the biblical and Jewish meaning (anamnesis).**

In **Jewish liturgical tradition**, anamnesis means to **make present** a past event in a real, active way. It's not merely symbolic or nostalgic—it's **participatory.**

This is especially clear in the **Passover**, where each Jewish family doesn't just remember the Exodus—they **relive it.** Even today, during the Passover meal, Jews say:

"It is because of what the LORD did for me when I came out of Egypt" (Exodus 13:8).

They speak **as if they themselves were there**, because in Jewish liturgy, remembrance is **real participation** in God's saving acts.

What This Means for the Eucharist

When Jesus says, **"Do this in remembrance (anamnesis) of Me,"** He is not commanding a symbolic memorial. **He is instituting a New Passover**—one in which we **participate** in His once-for-all sacrifice at Calvary, made present in the Eucharist.

This is why the Church teaches that the Mass is not a re-crucifixion but a **re-presentation** of the one sacrifice of Christ, transcending time and space. The past event is made **sacramentally present**.

Supporting Scripture

- **Hebrews 10:3** uses anamnesis when speaking of Old Testament sacrifices as a "reminder" of sin—but Jesus' sacrifice, once for all, fulfills what those sacrifices pointed toward.

- **1 Corinthians 11:24–25**–Paul echoes Jesus: "Do this in remembrance of me" (anamnesis), emphasizing the sacrificial and covenantal nature of the Eucharist.

In Summary

- **Anamnesis** = remembrance that is **active**, **liturgical**, and **sacramental**.

- At Mass, we don't just remember the Cross—we **enter into it**.

- The Eucharist is the **New Covenant Passover**, and remembrance means **making present** the saving act of Christ.

The Missing Fourth Cup

- **A traditional Jewish Passover meal had four cups of wine**, but Jesus stops after the third cup at the Last Supper.

- Instead of drinking the final cup, He says:

"I will not drink again of the fruit of the vine until the kingdom of God comes" (Luke 22:18).

- On the Cross, Jesus drinks wine (John 19:29–30) and says, "It is finished," completing the New Passover and revealing the Mass as the New Covenant Passover meal.

For more on this, see Scott Hahn's *The Fourth Cup*.

The Manna in the Desert: The Eucharist as the True Bread from Heaven

- In Exodus 16, God provides manna (bread from heaven) to sustain Israel in the desert.

- This prefigures Jesus as the true Bread of Life:

  "Your ancestors ate manna in the desert, and they died. But the bread that comes down from heaven gives eternal life… The bread that I will give is My flesh" (John 6:49–51).

- Just as Israel depended on manna for physical survival, **we depend on the Eucharist for spiritual life.**

The Bread of the Presence (*Lehem haPanim*)

- In the Temple of Jerusalem, priests placed twelve loaves of sacred bread before God as an everlasting covenant (Leviticus 24:5-9).

- This "Bread of the Presence" was:

  1. **Placed in the Holy of Holies** → The Eucharist is the Real Presence of Christ.

  2. **Eaten by the priests** → In the New Covenant, all believers are a "royal priesthood" (1 Peter 2:9).

3. **A sign of God's covenant** → Jesus calls the Eucharist "the new covenant in My blood" (Luke 22:20).

The Sacrifice of Melchizedek

- In Genesis 14:18, the mysterious priest-king Melchizedek offers bread and wine in thanksgiving.

- Melchizedek's offering **foreshadows** Jesus' priesthood, as **confirmed** in Hebrews 7:17.

- Jesus, like Melchizedek, offers bread and wine, but in the Eucharist, it **becomes** His Body and Blood.

Isaiah's Prophecy of the Messianic Banquet

- Isaiah 25:6–9 describes a heavenly banquet where God will provide a feast:

   "On this mountain the Lord Almighty will prepare a feast of rich food, a banquet of aged wine… He will swallow up death forever."

- **Jesus fulfills this in the Eucharistic banquet**, where we partake of His Body and Blood, which conquer death.

The Eucharist and Jewish Sacrifice

- **In the Old Testament**, atonement required a blood sacrifice (Leviticus 17:11).

- **In the New Covenant**, Jesus offers Himself as the final sacrifice (Hebrews 9:12–14).

- **The Eucharist makes this sacrifice present at every Mass**, just as Jewish sacrifices were continually re-presented.

John 6: The Eucharist Is Literal, Not Metaphorical

When we look closely at **John 6**, it's clear: Jesus taught that the Eucharist is **literal**, not symbolic. Far from softening His words when people protested, Jesus **doubled down**—especially by using the Greek word *trogo*, which means to **gnaw or chew** like an animal. (For deeper study, see *The Lamb's Supper* by Scott Hahn and *Jesus and the Jewish Roots of the Eucharist* by Brant Pitre.)

The Feeding of the 5,000 (John 6:1–15)

Before He even begins teaching about the Bread of Life, Jesus works a **Eucharistic foreshadowing** miracle: the multiplication of the loaves and fishes. The crowd is amazed and wants to make Him king (John 6:15), but Jesus withdraws—because His mission isn't about earthly food or political power. This miraculous feeding prepares the way for a far greater gift that Jesus will offer: **His very own flesh in the Eucharist**.

Jesus Introduces the Bread of Life (John 6:26–40)

The next day, the crowds find Jesus in Capernaum and demand another sign (John 6:25). Jesus challenges them, saying:

"Do not work for food that perishes, but for food that endures for eternal life" (John 6:27).

They want more earthly bread; Jesus points to **heavenly bread—Himself.**

"I am the bread of life; whoever comes to me will never hunger, and whoever believes in me will never thirst" (John 6:35).

At this point, Jesus is speaking about **believing in Him** spiritually. **But then He shifts—and the shift is critical.**

Jesus Reiterates: "Eat my flesh, drink my blood" (John 6:51–58).

Jesus then takes it much further, saying: *"The bread that I will give is my flesh for the life of the world"* (John 6:51).

The Jews are shocked and protest: *"How can this man give us his flesh to eat?"* (John 6:52)

If Jesus were speaking symbolically, this would have been the perfect moment to correct them.

But He doesn't.

Instead, He **intensifies His language**:

"Amen, amen, I say to you, unless you eat the flesh of the Son of Man and drink his blood, you have no life in you" (John 6:53).

The Key Greek Word: "*Trogo*" (To Gnaw or Chew)

Initially, Jesus uses the common Greek word *phago* (φαγω), meaning simply "to eat."

But when the crowd objects, **He switches to an even stronger word: *trogo* (τρώγω).**

Trogo means to **gnaw, crunch, or chew like an animal eating raw meat.** This word is **never used metaphorically** in Greek—it always refers to literal, physical eating.

Jesus could have softened His message. Instead, He makes it more graphic, not less.

He repeats *trogo* **four times:**

- **John 6:54**–"Whoever gnaws (trogo) my flesh and drinks my blood has eternal life."

- **John 6:56**–"Whoever gnaws (trogo) my flesh remains in me."

- **John 6:57**–"Whoever gnaws (trogo) will live because of me."

- **John 6:58**–"Whoever gnaws (trogo) this bread will live forever."

If Jesus were speaking symbolically, **using such a shocking word—and repeating it four times—would make no sense.**

The Reaction: Many Disciples Leave (John 6:60–66)

Hearing this, even many of His own disciples say: *"This saying is hard; who can accept it?"* (John 6:60)

Instead of softening His words or offering a symbolic explanation, **Jesus allows them to struggle.**

Then comes one of the saddest verses in Scripture: *"As a result of this, many of His disciples returned to their former way of life and no longer accompanied Him"* (John 6:66).

It wasn't just a few individuals who walked away from Jesus after His Bread of Life discourse—it was **thousands.** The Gospel tells us that Jesus had just fed over **5,000 men**, not counting women and children (John 6:10), and many of these same followers sought Him out the next day (John 6:24–26). When Jesus taught that they must eat His flesh and drink His blood, **the vast majority** could not accept it and abandoned Him (John 6:66). This mass departure shows just how shocking and demanding His teaching was—**and how seriously He meant it.**

If Jesus had been speaking symbolically, He would have clarified. Instead, He let them go, because He meant exactly what He said. **If this were only a metaphor, why would they walk away?**

And **why wouldn't Jesus call them back to explain?**

Instead, He turns to the Twelve and asks: *"Do you also want to leave?"* (John 6:67)

Peter's Response: Faith Over Understanding (John 6:68–69)

Though confused, Peter responds with faith: *"Lord, to whom shall we go? You have the words of eternal life"* (John 6:68).

Even if Peter doesn't fully understand yet, **he trusts Jesus**—because truth comes from Christ, even when it is difficult. So ask yourself, are you one of the crowd who walks away from Jesus or do you trust and follow Him, even if you don't fully understand, like Peter?

The Last Supper Confirms John 6 (Matthew 26:26–28)

The full meaning of John 6 is revealed at the **Last Supper**: *"Take and eat; this IS my body... Drink from it, all of you, for this IS my blood"* (Matthew 26:26–28).

Jesus **does not say** "this represents my body" or "this symbolizes my blood." He says IS—and the Apostles no longer object. They now understand that Jesus meant exactly what He said in John 6.

And remember, when Jesus says, *"Do this in remembrance of me"* (Luke 22:19), the Greek word for "remembrance" is **anamnesis**—which doesn't mean a mere mental recall. It means to **make a past event truly present and effective now**. In the Eucharist, the once-for-all sacrifice of Christ is **made present**—not re-sacrificed, but made truly real and accessible to us through the miracle of the Mass.

Because **God is outside of time**, the sacrifice of Calvary and the offering of the Last Supper are not events trapped in the past; they are eternally alive before the Father. Every time the Eucharist is celebrated, **heaven and earth unite**, and we are mystically present at the foot of the Cross and at the table of the Last Supper. The veil between time and eternity is pierced, and we are truly with Jesus—at Calvary, at the Last Supper, and at the heavenly banquet—offering and receiving the perfect sacrifice of love.

The Early Church Believed in the Real Presence

The earliest Christians understood John 6 **literally**, not symbolically. They were willing to suffer and **die** for this belief in the Real Presence:

- **St. Ignatius of Antioch (107 AD):**

  "The Eucharist is the flesh of our Savior Jesus Christ." (*Letter to the Smyrnaeans*)

- **St. Justin Martyr (150 AD):**

  "We do not receive these as common bread and drink, but as Jesus Christ, who became flesh."

- **St. Cyril of Jerusalem (350 AD):**

  "Do not doubt whether this is true, but take the words of the Savior in faith; He is the Truth, He cannot lie."

If the Eucharist were merely symbolic, why would the early Christians **face persecution and martyrdom** rather than deny it?

John 6 remains one of the strongest proofs for the Catholic teaching on the Eucharist. There are times when Scripture is speaking metaphorically, but this isn't one of those times. Here in John 6 Jesus **spoke literally**—and the Church has faithfully preserved and proclaimed this truth ever since.

Conclusion: The Eucharist as the Fulfillment of Jewish Worship and the Living Heart of the New Covenant

The Eucharist is not just a symbol. It is the New Passover, the center of Christian worship, and the fulfillment of everything the Old Covenant foreshadowed. Jesus Christ is the true Passover Lamb, sacrificed for our salvation. Just as the Israelites had to **eat the lamb** to be spared from death during the first Passover, so too must we **consume the Lamb**

93

of God in the Eucharist to share in His life. The Last Supper and the Crucifixion are not two separate events—they are **one continuous sacrifice**, transcending time and space. God, who exists outside of time, makes the once-for-all sacrifice of Calvary **present** at every Mass.

This Eucharistic reality is prefigured all throughout the Old Testament. The manna in the wilderness pointed to the true bread from heaven. The Bread of the Presence in the Tabernacle foreshadowed the Real Presence of Christ. Melchizedek's offering of bread and wine anticipated the priesthood and the Eucharistic sacrifice. Isaiah's vision of the heavenly banquet revealed the eternal feast offered now at every Catholic altar. Every Old Testament sacrifice finds its perfect and final fulfillment in Christ, whose offering is not repeated, but **re-presented** at each and every Mass in a sacramental and real way. The Mass is not a mere memorial; it is **a true sacrifice**. The Eucharist is not simply bread and wine; it is **Jesus Christ Himself**—fully present, Body, Blood, Soul, and Divinity. When we receive the Eucharist, we are united to the living Lamb of God who takes away the sins of the world. This is the profound meaning behind Christ's command:

"Do this in remembrance of Me" (Luke 22:19).

In Greek, the word for "remembrance" is **anamnesis**, and in Hebrew, it is **zikkaron**—both terms meaning far more than simply recalling a past event. Anamnesis means to make a past reality truly present and effective now. The Eucharist is the anamnesis—**the living memorial**—of the New Covenant, the real making present of Christ's sacrifice. In the Mass, we are drawn into the one sacrifice of Calvary, not watching from a distance, but **participating in it**. It is through the Eucharist that we are spiritually nourished, transformed, and bound together as one Body in Christ.

The Eucharist is not only the fulfillment of Jewish worship—it is the fulfillment of every longing of the human heart for union with God. **It is Jesus Himself, truly with us, until the end of the age**.

"I came to realize that the Church is not a man-made institution, but the family of God, and the Eucharist is not just symbolic, but truly Jesus Himself."

—Kimberly Hahn (wife of former Protestant Pastor, Dr. Scott Hahn)

Divine Evidence:
Eucharistic Miracles, the Shroud, and Apparitions of Mary

Every now and then, God pulls back the veil between heaven and earth in a dramatic way—offering not just spiritual consolation but **physical proof**. Eucharistic miracles are among the most astonishing signs He has given to affirm what the Church has always taught: that Jesus Christ is truly present—Body, Blood, Soul, and Divinity—in the Eucharist. These aren't pious legends or symbolic visions. In multiple, well-documented cases across centuries and continents, consecrated hosts have transformed into visible human flesh and blood, **often under rigorous scientific scrutiny**.

What's more astounding is what modern science has revealed about these miracles. In cases like Lanciano (Italy), Buenos Aires (Argentina), and Tixtla (Mexico), the transformed Eucharist has been analyzed by independent pathologists and laboratories—often without revealing the source of the sample. The results have been consistent and shocking: the tissue is human heart muscle, from the left ventricle, under extreme duress. The blood type is AB—the same as found on the Shroud of Turin. **The DNA shows characteristics that cannot be explained by contamination or fraud**. These findings are not easily dismissed, even by skeptical scientists.

Far from being mere curiosities, these miracles point us back to the very heart of Catholic worship: the Eucharist. They are divine exclamation points that echo Christ's own words in John 6: "My flesh is true food, and my blood is true drink." In a world hungry for proof and longing for something real, these supernatural events challenge us to see with the eyes of faith—and to fall to our knees in reverent awe. This chapter will explore some of the most powerful Eucharistic miracles and what they reveal about the love, mercy, and Real Presence of Jesus in the Blessed Sacrament.

What Are Eucharistic Miracles?

Eucharistic miracles occur when, during or after the consecration at Mass, the host (which is the Body of Christ) exhibits physical signs of Christ's presence—such as bleeding, transforming into human tissue, or remaining miraculously preserved for centuries.

These miracles are not legends; many have been thoroughly investigated by medical and scientific experts, often with no natural explanation.

The Most Famous Eucharistic Miracles:

1. Lanciano, Italy (eighth century)

- A priest doubting the Real Presence saw the host turn into living flesh and the wine become visible blood during Mass. The miraculous flesh was preserved for centuries, allowing it to be scientifically analyzed in the 1970s where scientific studies revealed:

  - The flesh was confirmed to be human heart tissue (myocardium).

  - The blood was type AB, the universal plasma recipient.

  - The tissues had no preservatives yet were perfectly preserved for over 1,200 years.

2. Buenos Aires, Argentina (1996)

- A consecrated host was found on the ground, placed in water to dissolve (a standard practice), but instead it turned into bloody tissue.

- In 2005, scientists discovered:

  - The tissue was living human heart muscle, from a person under severe stress.

  - The blood type was AB, identical to Lanciano's.

  - The white blood cells were active, meaning the sample was from living tissue, despite having no oxygen source for years.

3. Sokolka, Poland (2008)

- A host accidentally dropped and left to dissolve was found to contain heart muscle tissue, merging inseparably with the bread at a molecular level.

- Scientists concluded it was myocardial tissue from a living human being, with the same AB blood type.

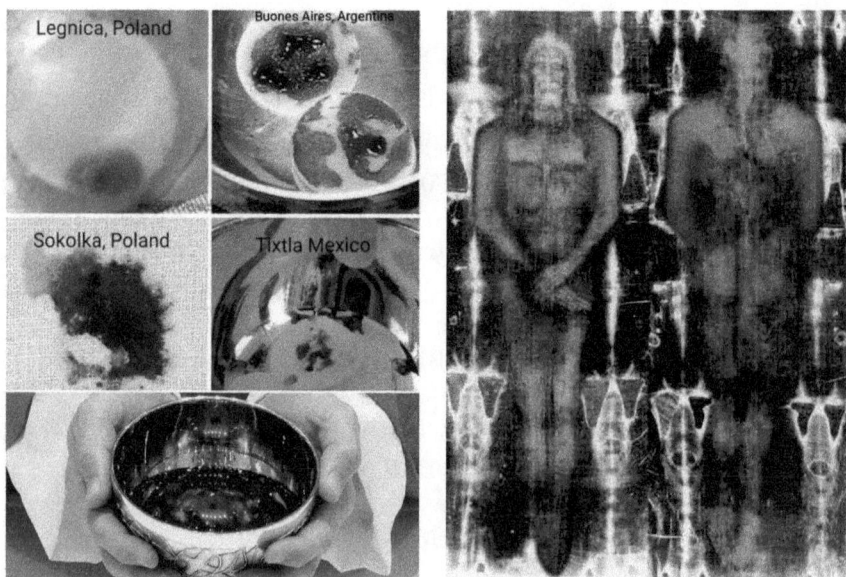

Connection to the Shroud of Turin

The Shroud of Turin, believed to be the burial cloth of Jesus, has been the subject of extensive scientific study, and **much of the evidence supports its authenticity**. The image on the cloth is not painted, dyed, or scorched—it is a 3D photographic negative, with details of a crucified man consistent with Roman execution methods, including wounds from scourging, nails in the wrists, and a crown of thorns. Advanced analysis has shown pollen from Jerusalem and a type of limestone found only near the tombs of that region. While some carbon dating tests have been debated, new research shows those results were skewed by medieval repairs to the corner of cloth that had been burned in a fire. The Shroud remains one of the most studied and mysterious artifacts in human history—**and science continues to affirm that it is not a forgery** but a powerful witness to the Passion of Christ.

What Did Scientists Find?

- The blood on the Shroud is human, type AB.

- This is the same blood type found in multiple Eucharistic miracles! (see Real Presence Eucharistic Education and Adoration Association)

- AB is also the blood type most common among people of Middle Eastern descent, which fits Jesus' ethnicity and indicates his likely blood type.

- The blood shows signs of trauma and torture, consistent with crucifixion.

Historically & Anatomically:

Roman crucifixions typically involved **nailing through the wrists**, not the palms, because:

- **The palm cannot support body weight**—nails through the hands alone would tear through the flesh.

- **The wrist area (between the radius and ulna bones)** could support the body's weight, especially if nailed through a spot known as **Destot's space**.

- The Greek word used for *"hand"* (*cheir*, χείρ) in the New Testament can refer to the entire lower arm, including the wrist.

  The **Shroud of Turin** shows nail wounds in the **wrists**, not the palms. This matches what we know about Roman crucifixion techniques.

What Does This Mean?

These miracles powerfully affirm what Jesus taught in John 6:

> "My flesh is true food, and my blood is true drink... unless you eat the flesh of the Son of Man and drink His blood, you have no life in you."

Marian Apparitions:

Our Lady of Guadalupe (Mexico, 1531)

- **Visionary:** St. Juan Diego

- **Miracle:** Image of Our Lady imprinted on tilma (cloak), which remains **miraculously preserved** for nearly 500 years; scientifically inexplicable.

- **Message:** Call to conversion and faith in her Son; affirmed the dignity of the native peoples.

- **Eucharistic Connection:** She appeared during the early evangelization of the Americas, helping usher in a massive conversion to Catholicism—and with it, the reception of the Sacraments, especially the Eucharist.

- **Impact:** Over **9 million conversions** in less than a decade.

Our Lady of Lourdes (France, 1858)

- **Visionary:** St. Bernadette Soubirous

- **Miracle:** A spring with healing waters appeared at Mary's request; thousands have reported miraculous cures.

- **Message:** Call to prayer, penance, and devotion to the Immaculate Conception.

- **Eucharistic Connection:** Lourdes emphasizes confession, prayer, and Eucharistic adoration—core parts of every pilgrimage there.

Our Lady of Fatima (Portugal, 1917)

- **Visionaries:** Lucia, Francisco, and Jacinta

- **Miracles:** The **Miracle of the Sun**, witnessed by over **70,000 people**, including skeptics and journalists.

- **Message:** Repentance, the Rosary, consecration to her Immaculate Heart, and reparation for sins—especially those against the Eucharist and purity.

- **Eucharistic Connection:** In 1916 (the year before the Marian apparitions), an **angel appeared with the Eucharist,** teaching the children a profound prayer of Eucharistic reparation:

- *"Most Holy Trinity, I adore You profoundly..."*

- **Prophecies Fulfilled:** WWII, rise of communism, and the assassination attempt on Pope John Paul II.

Our Lady of Akita (Japan, 1973)

- **Visionary:** Sr. Agnes Sasagawa

- **Miracle:** A statue of Mary wept human tears 101 times; tested by scientists and confirmed genuine.

- **Message:** Similar to Fatima—warnings about sin, suffering, and the need for prayer, especially the Rosary.

- **Eucharistic Connection:** Emphasis on the **sacrifice of the Mass**, reverence for the Eucharist, and spiritual protection against apostasy.

Common Themes Across Apparitions

1. **Call to Eucharistic Devotion**–Mary always points us to her Son, especially present in the Eucharist.

2. **Emphasis on Repentance and Reparation**–For sins against the Sacred Heart of Jesus and the Eucharist.

3. **The Rosary as a Weapon**–Spiritual protection and participation in Christ's victory.

4. **Signs and Wonders**–Healings, conversions, miracles of the sun, unexplainable preservation of relics.

How the Church Investigates Apparitions

The Vatican applies rigorous criteria before approving an apparition:

- The messages must be **doctrinally sound** (no heresy).

- The person receiving them must be **mentally stable**, morally upright, and not seeking fame or gain.

- There must be **positive spiritual fruits**: increased prayer, conversions, vocations, and return to the Sacraments.

- Any miracles associated must be **verifiable and scientifically inexplicable.**

Only a small number of apparitions receive official approval. Others may remain under investigation or be rejected if found inauthentic or harmful.

Why This Matters in the Larger Picture

Like Eucharistic miracles and the Shroud of Turin, **Marian apparitions serve as divine "interruptions" of the ordinary**, reminding us that God is not distant. Through Mary, heaven calls us back to her Son, especially through the Sacraments of Confession and the Eucharist. These events aren't about emotional mysticism—they're consistent, verifiable signs that **God still speaks**, and He often sends His mother to prepare the way.

Conclusion: These Miracles Strongly Support the Catholic Faith

The Eucharist is not just a symbol—it is the Real Presence of Jesus Christ: Body, Blood, Soul, and Divinity. Through the centuries, God has not left us to rely on faith alone; He has given us tangible signs—Eucharistic miracles where the consecrated host has turned into actual human flesh and blood, **matching the very tissues of a living, suffering heart.** And in the Shroud of Turin, we find a silent yet powerful witness to the Passion, death, and Resurrection of Jesus—preserved in the burial cloth of a crucified man who bears all the marks described in the Gospels.

Science can study the evidence, but it cannot fully explain it. These miracles are not meant to replace faith but to confirm it—to awaken us to the profound reality that what happens on the altar is no mere ritual. **It is Calvary made present again.**

If the Eucharist is Jesus—and these signs affirm that it is—then we are standing on holy ground every time we approach the altar. These miraculous reminders invite us to believe more deeply, worship more reverently, and receive Him more worthily.

The God who once walked among us still does—veiled in bread and wine, yet truly present. He leaves traces not just in history, but in the very elements, so that we might know: *This is My Body, given for you.*

Remember, even many who witnessed his miracles firsthand and saw him face-to-face walked away in unbelief.

The **Shroud of Turin**, **Eucharistic miracles**, and **Marian apparitions** are not isolated phenomena—they are threads of the same divine tapestry. In them, God is reaching out in a distinct way to a distracted world: *Come home. I am real. I am here. I am with you always.*

These signs are gentle hands pointing us toward the Sacraments, the Church, and above all… the **Eucharistic Christ**, waiting for us in every Catholic tabernacle.

For a deeper dive on this topic, see references on pages 211-213.

Heaven Hears Us:
A Biblical Case for the Intercession of Saints

One of the most misunderstood aspects of Catholicism—especially by those outside the Church—is our relationship with the saints and, most notably, with Mary. Protestants often accuse Catholics of "worshiping" Mary or the saints, believing that any prayer directed to them must be idolatry. But this claim reflects a misunderstanding not just of Catholic teaching but of worship itself.

In biblical and historical terms, **worship involves sacrifice**—and sacrifice is reserved for God alone. Catholics offer sacrifice only to God, most fully in the Mass, which is the re-presentation of Christ's once-for-all sacrifice on Calvary (Hebrews 9:26–28). What we offer to saints is not worship (*latria*) but **veneration** (*dulia*)—a deep honor and reverence. Mary, as the Mother of God, receives a unique honor (*hyperdulia*)—but never worship.

When Catholics "pray to" saints, we are not worshiping them—we are asking for their **intercession**. Just as you might ask a friend or pastor to pray for you, we ask our brothers and sisters in heaven—who are **more alive than we are** (Luke 20:38)—to pray on our behalf. Scripture affirms the power of intercessory prayer: "The prayer of a righteous man is powerful and effective" (James 5:16). And Revelation gives us a striking image of the saints in heaven offering our prayers before God like incense (Revelation 5:8; 8:3–4). Intercession is not a distraction from Jesus—it is one part of the Body of Christ lifting up another.

The Communion of Saints: A Biblical Reality

Catholics believe in the **communion of saints**—the idea that all Christians, whether on earth or in heaven, remain united in Christ:

- *Hebrews 12:1*–"Since we are surrounded by so great a cloud of witnesses, let us rid ourselves of every burden and sin."

- *Romans 8:38–39*–"Neither death nor life... will be able to separate us from the love of God in Christ Jesus our Lord."

Death does not sever the unity of the Church—it deepens it. The saints in heaven are not "dead" in the sense of being disconnected. They are **glorified members of the same Body** to which we still belong.

Heavenly Intercession in Scripture

Scripture is not silent about the activity of the saints in heaven. In fact, it shows them **actively interceding for us**:

- *Revelation 5:8*–"The twenty-four elders fell down before the Lamb... holding golden bowls full of incense, which are the prayers of the saints."

- *Revelation 8:3–4*–"The smoke of the incense, with the prayers of the saints, went up before God from the angel's hand."

The prayers of the saints are presented before the throne of God—clearly showing that intercessory prayer continues beyond death.

Why Ask for Mary's Intercession?

Mary plays a unique role—not just because she is the Mother of Jesus, but because she **participated in salvation history** like no other creature. Her Fiat ("Let it be done to me according to your word"–Luke 1:38) opened the door to the Incarnation. And her role didn't end there:

At the **Wedding at Cana**, Mary interceded on behalf of the people, saying simply, "They have no wine." Jesus' reply seems dismissive—but He performs the miracle anyway. And He does so **immediately after Mary says to the servants, "Do whatever He tells you"** (John 2:1–11). Mary's intercession sparked Jesus' first public miracle.

If she could intercede with that kind of power on earth, how much more in heaven, glorified in union with Him?

At the Cross, Jesus gave Mary to the Church: "Woman, behold your son... Behold your mother" (John 19:26–27).

The Church has always understood this moment as more than personal care. Mary was given to us as our spiritual mother—just as John received her, so do we.

But Isn't Jesus the Only Mediator? (1 Timothy 2:5)

Yes, Jesus is the only Mediator of salvation between man and God the Father. Only through His sacrifice are we redeemed and reconciled to the Father. No saint, no priest, no prayer partner can **replace** the saving mediation of Christ.

However, there are many mediators between us and Jesus Himself—helpers, intercessors, and fellow members of His Body. **If asking friends and family to pray for you is not a violation of Christ's unique role (and it isn't), then neither is asking someone already perfected in heaven.**

In fact, Scripture commands earthly Christians to intercede for one another: 1 Timothy 2:1–"I urge that supplications, prayers, intercessions, and thanksgivings be made for all people."

Paul encourages intercessory prayer precisely because God desires to work through His Body to bless and build up His people. **The saints, being fully alive in Christ, continue this role glorified.**

If we on earth can pray for each other without undermining Jesus' role, then the glorified saints—perfected and close to the throne of God—can pray for us **even more powerfully**. Thus, the saints' intercession magnifies the work of Christ. It does not compete with it.

The Early Church Asked for the Saints' Intercession

This isn't some late Catholic invention. The earliest Christians—just a generation or two after the apostles—openly asked for the saints' intercession:

- **St. Cyril of Jerusalem (c. 350 AD):**

  "We then commemorate also those who have fallen asleep before us… that at their prayers and intercessions God would receive our supplication."

- **St. Augustine (c. 400 AD):**

  "The saints in heaven help us by their prayers."

These men weren't confused pagans. They were bishops and defenders of the apostolic faith. And they **clearly believed** in the power of heavenly intercession.

Catholics Worship Only God

Let's be clear on terms:

- **Latria**–Worship due to God alone

- **Dulia**–Honor due to saints

- **Hyperdulia**–Special veneration due to Mary as the Mother of God

Catholics do not—and never have—**worshiped** Mary or the saints.

That accusation is a misunderstanding of both Catholic teaching and biblical terminology.

Conclusion: The Saints Point Us to Christ

The Catholic practice of asking saints to intercede for us is not just ancient—it's profoundly biblical. The saints are alive in Christ, standing before His throne, offering our prayers like incense. Mary is not a distraction from Jesus—she is His first disciple and greatest witness. Her words at Cana still echo: **"Do whatever He tells you."**

When we ask for the intercession of the saints, we are not bypassing Jesus. We are **leaning into the reality of the Body of Christ**, which is not limited by death. We are surrounded by a great cloud of witnesses—and their prayers lift us toward heaven.

As the early Christians believed, so do we: We are one family, one Church, one Body—on earth and in heaven—united in Jesus Christ. And just as we pray for one another now, the saints in glory do not stop loving or praying for the Church they are still part of.

Faith, Works, and Salvation: What Do Catholics Actually Believe?

Few topics generate more confusion (and strawman arguments) between Catholics and Protestants than the question of salvation and good works. One of the most frequent accusations hurled at the Catholic Church is that it teaches a "works-based salvation," as if we believe heaven is earned through human effort or religious performance. **But this isn't just a distortion—it's flat-out false**. The Catholic Church has never taught that we can merit salvation simply by our works. Most of these critiques don't come from people who've read the *Catechism of the Catholic Church (CCC)*, but from those repeating secondhand claims or reacting to Catholic language without understanding it.

The Catechism clearly states:

"Our justification comes from the grace of God. Grace is favor, the free and undeserved help that God gives us to respond to His call to become children of God..." (CCC 1996).

The Catholic view of salvation affirms grace as the starting point, sustaining power, and ultimate cause of our redemption. What we believe about faith and works isn't man-made legalism—it's deeply biblical, historically rooted, and consistent with how the early Church lived the Gospel.

The Catholic Church affirms, without hesitation, that salvation is a free gift of God's grace. We are saved by grace through faith (Ephesians 2:8–9), not by any merit of our own. But unlike many Protestant interpretations, Catholic teaching also embraces the **full**

scope of Scripture, which tells us that **faith must be alive and active**—expressed through love (Galatians 5:6), obedience (Romans 6:16), and perseverance (Matthew 24:13). Works do not *earn* salvation—they are the *fruit* of salvation. They are the evidence of a life transformed by grace, the way we respond to the free gift we've received.

It's also important to understand that when Scripture criticizes "works of the law," **it's not condemning good deeds or acts of love**—it's referring to the ceremonial and ritual observances of the Old Covenant. In contrast, the "works" upheld in Catholic theology are works of charity, humility, and cooperation with God's grace—empowered by the Holy Spirit, not by human strength. This chapter will carefully unpack what the Church actually teaches about salvation, how grace and free will interact, and why **faith and works are not enemies**—but two sides of the same coin in the life of a disciple.

Let's set the record straight on **what the Church actually teaches:**

We are saved by grace. Through faith. In Christ. But that grace is not just a legal declaration—it's a **transforming gift** that we must cooperate with through faith and love.

Here's the Catholic formula:

- We are saved by grace alone,
  (Ephesians 2:8–9)

- Through faith that is alive and working through love,
  (Galatians 5:6, James 2:24)

- As we persevere in obedience, by the power of the Holy Spirit.
  (Philippians 2:12–13, Matthew 10:22)

We don't **earn salvation**—we receive it as a gift. But like any gift, we must **accept it, respond to it,** and **live in it.** That response includes both faith and obedience.

Faith and Works: A False Either/Or

The Protestant Reformation emphasized "faith alone" (*sola fide*), but Scripture doesn't teach that we are saved by faith **alone**. In fact, the **only place in the Bible that uses the phrase "faith alone" is James 2:24**:

> **"You see that a person is justified by works and not by faith alone."**

This doesn't mean we earn salvation by works. It means that **true faith is never alone**—it always bears fruit in love, obedience, and good works of love, not works of the law. (John 15:5–6).

Cooperating with Grace

The Church teaches that **we must cooperate** with God's grace. That doesn't mean we save ourselves—it means **we freely respond** to the grace He gives. We're not co-saviors; we're **participants** in the saving work God has already accomplished, choosing to receive and walk in what Christ alone has made possible.

Think of it like this:

- A drowning person doesn't *rescue themselves.*

- But if a lifeguard throws them a rope, they still have to grab it.

- That act of grabbing the rope isn't "earning" salvation—it's **responding to the help they could never initiate on their own.**

Catechism of the Catholic Church (CCC) on Salvation

- **CCC 1996**– *"Our justification comes from the grace of God. Grace is favor, the free and undeserved help that God gives us."*

- **CCC 2008**– *"The merit of man before God in the Christian life* *arises from the fact that God has freely chosen to associate man with the work of his grace."*

- **CCC 2010**–*"Since the initiative belongs to God in the order of grace, no one can merit the initial grace of forgiveness and justification... Moved by the Holy Spirit, we can then merit for ourselves and for others the graces needed for sanctification."*

In short:

- **Initial justification is 100% God's work.**

- Our ongoing cooperation is also by **His grace**, not our own strength.

- Good works are not the cause of salvation—they are the **fruit** of a life in Christ.

So What About Works?

Good works matter—not because they earn salvation, but because they are **evidence of living faith**.

- **Matthew 25:31–46**–The sheep and the goats are judged based on what they *did*.

- **John 14:15**–"If you love Me, keep My commandments."

- **James 2:17**–"Faith by itself, if it does not have works, is dead."

Just as a healthy tree naturally bears fruit, a soul united to Christ will naturally live out love, generosity, repentance, and obedience.

When Scripture says we are not justified by "works of the law" (see Romans 3:28, Galatians 2:16), it's not condemning all good works— it's specifically referring to the **observances and legal requirements** of the Old Covenant, such as circumcision, dietary laws, and purity codes. St. Paul is clear: **we are no longer under the Mosaic Law**—we are under **the law of Christ**, which is the **law of love** (Galatians 6:2, Romans 13:8–10). Catholics believe we are justified by grace through faith, and that true saving faith expresses itself in **works of love**, not ritual works of the old law. That's why Paul also says in Galatians 5:6: *"Neither circumcision nor uncircumcision counts for anything, but only faith working through love."* We're not saved by checking boxes—we're saved by being united to Jesus through His Church, and living out that union in love, including participation in the Sacraments. The "law of Christ" is not about legalism—it's about the transformation of the heart, which naturally leads to a life of sacrificial love. These are the "good works" we were **created in Christ Jesus to do** (Ephesians 2:10)—not to earn salvation, but to live it out.

Conclusion: Faith AND Works (of Love—Not Old Testament Law)

Catholics believe that salvation is by grace through faith. We do not believe in salvation by human effort or that we can "earn" our way to heaven. Rather, we believe that Jesus paid the full price, and our good works are the fruit of that saving grace at work within us. Works are not a payment for salvation—they are the joyful response of a life transformed by love.

Much of the confusion comes from **misunderstanding** Paul's use of the phrase "works of the law." In Scripture, **this refers not to good deeds or acts of love, but to the ceremonial and ritual laws of the Old Covenant—circumcision, dietary restrictions, and legal codes that were meant to prepare Israel for the Messiah**. Paul makes it clear that these no longer justify us. **But that doesn't mean works, in general, are irrelevant**. The New Testament repeatedly teaches that faith must be active, alive, and expressed in love. As Galatians 5:6 puts it, what matters is "faith working through love."

This is what Catholics believe: we are saved by grace, through a living

faith that bears fruit in works of love. James tells us plainly that "faith without works is dead" (James 2:26). And Jesus Himself describes the final judgment not by doctrine alone but by how we loved—whether we fed the hungry, clothed the naked, and cared for the least among us (Matthew 25:31–46). These are not the obsolete works of Mosaic Law but the visible evidence of grace alive in the soul.

Faith and works are not enemies; they are two sides of the same coin in the life of a believer. Grace transforms us, and love proves it.

The Last Four Things:
Death, Judgment, Heaven, and Hell

The Catholic Church teaches what tradition calls *The Last Four Things*: **Death, Judgment, Heaven, and Hell.** These aren't idyllic metaphors or theological scare tactics—they are eternal realities rooted in Scripture, affirmed by the Church Fathers, and echoed by the saints across centuries. They also answer the most pressing human question:

What happens when I die?

These teachings are not meant to paralyze us with fear but to awaken us to eternity, to clarify what's truly at stake in this life, and to prepare us for our final destiny.

Death: The Door We All Must Pass Through

"It is appointed for men to die once, and after that comes judgment" (Hebrews 9:27).

Death is not an accident or an interruption—it's part of the human condition after the Fall. Every soul must face it. For those outside the faith, death can seem terrifying, mysterious, or meaningless. But for the Christian, **death is not the end—it's a beginning.** It is the final purification of the soul and the passage into what we were made for: eternity.

Catholicism does not romanticize death, but it does rob it of its power. **Christ conquered death** through the Cross and Resurrection. Therefore, for the faithful soul in a state of grace, death is not a curse but the moment of meeting Christ face-to-face.

Judgment: Truth Revealed

The Church teaches two judgments:

- **The Particular Judgment**: Immediately after death, each soul stands before Christ and receives its eternal sentence—either heaven (directly or through purgatory) or hell.

- **The Final Judgment**: At the end of time, all souls are reunited with their bodies, and every deed, intention, and consequence is revealed before all creation. God's justice and mercy are fully vindicated.

"For we must all appear before the judgment seat of Christ" (2 Corinthians 5:10).

This is not divine cruelty—it is divine justice. Our lives matter. **Our choices echo into eternity**. Nothing is hidden from God, but everything will be healed, restored, or judged according to truth.

Heaven: The Fulfillment of Desire

"No eye has seen, no ear has heard, nor has it entered into the heart of man what God has prepared for those who love Him" (1 Corinthians 2:9).

Heaven is not a cloud-covered resting place with harps and halos. It is **union with God Himself**—the Beatific Vision. In heaven, the soul sees God face-to-face and is forever transformed by that vision. There is no more sorrow, no more fear, only perfect love, perfect knowledge, and perfect joy.

The Eastern Catholic and Orthodox Churches emphasize **theosis**—that we are not merely saved from sin but divinized by grace. "God became man so that man might become God," wrote St. Athanasius. Heaven is not only being with God—it is becoming like Him in love and glory. It is the complete fulfillment of the deepest hunger of the human heart.

Hell: Love Rejected, Truth Refused

"Depart from me, you cursed, into the eternal fire prepared for the devil and his angels" (Matthew 25:41).

Hell is not a myth, nor a temporary state. It is **a real and eternal separation from God, freely chosen by the soul** that refuses grace.

But here's the critical distinction: **the Catholic view of hell is not that of a divine sadist punishing people for failing a cosmic quiz.** Catholic theology sees hell as the tragic outcome of the soul's rejection of love itself. God desires all to be saved (1 Timothy 2:4), and He offers grace to everyone. But **love cannot be forced**—and some souls freely reject it.

As the Catechism says:

"To die in mortal sin without repenting and accepting God's merciful love means remaining separated from Him forever by our own free choice. This state of definitive self-exclusion from communion with God and the blessed is called 'hell.'" (CCC 1033)

Catholic vs. Protestant Views of Hell

Many Protestant traditions—especially fundamentalist or evangelical groups—tend to present **a courtroom model of salvation**: God is the cosmic judge, the Bible is the lawbook, and sinners are criminals who deserve eternal punishment unless they accept Jesus as their personal Savior.

This view often emphasizes **penal substitution**—the belief that Christ bore the punishment we deserve so God could legally forgive us. In this framework, hell is often portrayed as a **literal lake of fire**, where sinners are **consciously tortured** by God's wrath forever.

Catholicism, on the other hand, emphasizes **relational rupture** over legal penalty. Sin is not just breaking rules—it's wounding a relationship.

Hell is not merely punishment—it is the full and final consequence of choosing the self over God. And God does not cease to love the damned—**they simply can no longer receive His love**, having sealed their hearts against it.

The **Eastern Catholic** understanding goes even deeper: God's love is inescapable—**it is the experience of that love that becomes either heaven or hell**. For the saved, it is bliss. For the damned, it is torment—not because God changes, but because **they do not want Him**.

As St. Isaac the Syrian wrote in his *Ascetical Homilies*, particularly Homily 84, we find this core concept:

"I also maintain that those who are punished in Gehenna are scourged by the **scourge of love**. *Nay, but what is so bitter and vehement as the torment of love?* [...] It is wrong to imagine that sinners in hell are deprived of the love of God. Love is given to all, but it acts in the damned as suffering."

In short, **God is not a cosmic cop or cruel judge—He is a loving Father**. But He respects our freedom, even when we use it to walk away from Him forever.

What About Non-Catholics? Are They All Damned?

No. The Church *explicitly rejects* the notion that all non-Catholics are automatically going to hell.

While Jesus Christ is the *only* Savior and the Catholic Church is the *fullness* of the means of salvation, **God is not limited by sacraments the way we are**. The Catechism clearly teaches:

"Those who, through no fault of their own, do not know the Gospel of Christ or His Church, but who seek God with a sincere heart... may achieve eternal salvation." (CCC 847)

This is not universalism. Not all paths lead to heaven. But God alone judges hearts. If someone is saved, it is *through* Christ—even if they did not know Him explicitly. That's why evangelization still matters: to reject Christ knowingly is to reject the source of grace.

The Last Thing: Love Wins—but Only if You Choose It

The Last Four Things confront us with this truth: **God honors your freedom.** He will not force Himself on you—not in life, and not in death. Eternity is the final answer to the question you answer every day: *Do I want God?*

St. John of the Cross put it bluntly:

"In the evening of life, we will be judged on love alone."

The Sacraments—**especially the Eucharist and Confession**—are not nice spiritual extras. They are the divine means by which we are **conformed to Christ** and made ready for eternal communion with Him.

Death is coming.

Judgment is real.

But heaven is possible—and hell is avoidable.

God doesn't damn us. He calls, He pursues, He forgives, He waits.

But love, by its nature, must be free.

The choice is ours.

Saved By Fire:
The Final Purification of Love

When I was Protestant, I thought purgatory was an invented doc-trine—a medieval loophole that undermined the sufficiency of Christ's sacrifice. To me, it sounded like a second chance or, worse, a Catholic guilt trap designed to keep people uncertain about their salvation. What I didn't know is that **purgatory has deep biblical roots, was believed by the earliest Christians, and far from being something to fear, is actually a gift of God's mercy.**

Purgatory isn't a *rejection* of the Cross. It's one of the ways the fruits of the Cross are *applied*. It doesn't add to Christ's work—it applies it. As C.S. Lewis, a non-Catholic, once put it: *"Our souls demand purgatory, don't they?"*

What *Is* Purgatory?

Purgatory is not a second chance at heaven, nor is it a "middle ground" between heaven and hell. The Church teaches that **purgatory is the final purification for those who die in God's grace but are not yet perfected in holiness** (cf. CCC 1030–1031). They are heaven-bound but not yet ready to see God face-to-face, for "nothing unclean will enter [heaven]" (Revelation 21:27).

But purgatory is more than just a theological necessity—it's a deeply inti-mate act of divine mercy. Scripture tells us that Christ is the Bridegroom and the Church is His Bride (Ephesians 5:25–27; Revelation 19:7–9). And like any bride preparing for her wedding day, the Church must be **spotless, pure, and radiant** when she stands before her Bridegroom.

That's exactly what purgatory is: **the final purification of the soul** so we can be fully united with Christ in glory. It's not about wrath—it's about readiness. Purgatory is how God, in His mercy, prepares us to enter that perfect union. It is not a second chance—it is the final cleansing of those already saved but not yet perfected. In this light, purgatory isn't something to fear. It's the bridal chamber where every last wrinkle and blemish is washed away before the **eternal wedding feast**.

Purgatory isn't necessarily a place—it's a *state* of purification. And while we often speak of it in terms of time, **it may be experienced instantaneous** in eternity, where God acts outside of time as we know it. Some saints even suggested that a single touch of God's purifying love could do in a moment what might otherwise feel like years of cleansing fire.

It's not punishment—it's **transformation**. The soul, still carrying attachments, wounds, and the residual effects of sin, enters into a final encounter with God's holiness that strips away all that is not of Him. It's the fire of divine love, not wrath.

Purgatory is not only consistent with God's justice—**it's consistent with His love**. And that purifying work doesn't begin at death. **It begins now**. The path to holiness is not a one-time event but a lifelong process of pruning, refining, and sanctifying grace. The saints called this the **"purgative way"**—a stage of the spiritual life in which we are purified of sin, selfishness, and all that keeps us from perfect union with God. And it's a path that often includes suffering.

Scripture is clear that suffering isn't meaningless. It can be redemptive. But it becomes powerful only when united to the Cross of Christ. St. Paul expresses this mystery in one of the most striking verses of the New Testament:

*"Now I rejoice in my sufferings for your sake, and in my flesh **I complete what is lacking** in Christ's afflictions, for the sake of His body, that is, the Church."* —Colossians 1:24

At first glance, it may sound as if Paul is suggesting that Christ's sacrifice was incomplete. But that's not what he's saying. Jesus' suffering on the Cross was absolute and sufficient for our salvation—once for all (Hebrews 10:10). Nothing can be added to it. What is "lacking" is not power—but **participation.**

Christ has invited His Body—the Church—to share in His redemptive work. In His love, He allows our suffering to become **part of the story**. When we unite our pain, our sacrifices, and our trials to His Cross, they take on a supernatural weight. We are not passive observers of salvation—we are **active participants**, not in saving ourselves, but in cooperating with grace and being conformed to the image of Christ (Romans 8:17).

This is why the Church speaks of **"offering up" our sufferings**—for souls in purgatory, for the conversion of sinners, for the good of the Church. It's not superstition. It's Scripture.

And this is where purgatory comes full circle: the **final purification after death** is simply the continuation—and completion—of the purifying work that began during our earthly life. The more we surrender, the more we cooperate with grace now, the less we'll need to be purged later. Holiness isn't about avoiding suffering. It's about **offering suffering**—like Paul did—*"for the sake of His Body, the Church."*

Biblical Foundations for Purgatory

While the word *purgatory* isn't found in Scripture—neither is *Trinity*— **the concept is unmistakably present in both the Old and New Testaments.**

123

1 Corinthians 3:12–15:

St. Paul describes a judgment where "the fire will test what sort of work each one has done." Some will be saved, "but only as through fire." This fire does not condemn—the person is saved—but it **purifies**. This is not hell, which offers no hope of salvation. It's the purifying judgment of a saved soul.

Matthew 5:25–26:

Jesus warns that a person will not get out "until you have paid the last penny" in a kind of prison. The Church has long understood this as a reference to **temporal consequences of sin**—a debt that remains even after forgiveness. Again, this is not hell (from which no one escapes), but something temporary and purifying.

Hebrews 12:22–24:

We are told of "the spirits of the righteous made perfect." If the righteous are not yet perfect at death, there must be a process of final perfection. Purgatory answers this scriptural tension—**how can the imperfect righteous be made perfect to enter heaven?**

2 Maccabees 12:44–46:

In one of the clearest references, Judas Maccabeus and his men pray for their fallen soldiers so "that they might be freed from their sins." Scripture calls this "a holy and pious thought." Why pray for the dead if their fate is sealed? This only makes sense if there is a state after death in which souls can be helped. This passage was so problematic for the Reformers that **Martin Luther removed it—along with the entire Deuterocanon—from Protestant Bibles.**

Early Christian Witness: The Faith of the First Centuries

Purgatory was not a late innovation—it was the lived belief of the early Church. Prayers for the dead appear as early as the second century. **Christian tombs in the Roman catacombs (150–200 AD) are covered with inscriptions like "May you find refreshment" and "Pray for us, we pray for you."** The idea that the faithful departed benefit from our prayers was taken for granted.

- **St. Augustine** encouraged prayers and Masses for his deceased mother, Monica, and taught that purification after death was part of the Christian hope.

- **St. Gregory the Great** spoke of souls being purified by fire and even described a form of purgation that involved temporal suffering after death.

- **Tertullian**, writing in the early 200s, mentions Christians offering prayers for the dead on their birthdays into eternity.

This wasn't a strange custom—it was standard Christian practice. The belief in purgatory predates the formal biblical canon and was confirmed by centuries of Christian liturgy and devotion.

A God of Justice *and* Mercy

Purgatory makes sense only in light of two truths:

1. **God is perfectly holy**, and nothing impure can dwell with Him.

2. **God is perfectly merciful**, and He desires all to be saved.

But **if we die with unrepented venial sins, or with attachments to pride, anger, or impurity, how can we endure the perfect holiness of God?** Purgatory is how God purifies us—not out of anger but out of love.

It's not "works-based salvation." Salvation is by grace alone. But **sanc-tification—the process of becoming holy—can continue after death**, if needed. And what a mercy that is.

To be clear: purgatory is *only* for the saved. Hell is eternal separation. **Purgatory is final healing**. As Pope Benedict XVI put it, "Purgatory is the inward fire that purifies the soul and brings it to full union with God."

The Communion of Saints: We Can Help

Perhaps the most beautiful part of this doctrine is that **we can help the souls in purgatory**. The Church calls this the "communion of saints"—the unity of believers on earth, in purgatory, and in heaven. We are not separated by death. We can assist the suffering souls with:

- Our prayers

- Masses offered on their behalf

- Fasting and sacrifices united to Christ

- Indulgences (rightly understood and properly applied)

This is not spiritual bribery. It is **love in action**—one body helping another, like a healthy limb compensating for an injured one.

Conclusion: A Gift of Mercy; Purified for Glory

If you died today, would your soul be perfect? Completely free from pride, selfishness, impatience, or the residue of sin? For most of us, the honest answer is **no**. And that's why purgatory is not something to fear—it's something to thank God for.

Purgatory is not a betrayal of the Gospel or a denial of Christ's suffi-ciency; it's the **radical extension of His mercy**. It reveals a God who doesn't just forgive sin but **heals the wounds** it leaves behind. A God who desires us not only to be saved—but to be **perfectly united to Him in love**.

Purgatory is **the final gift** for the imperfectly holy—a refining fire that purifies the soul and prepares it to enter the unimaginable glory of heaven. It's not punishment—it's love, finishing its work.

It is hope for the struggling.

It is healing for the wounded.

It is mercy for the saved.

And best of all, it means heaven is certain for those who pass through it. We are not left clinging to our brokenness. We are made whole, by love and through love, for love. Purgatory isn't something to dread. **It's the place where love burns away every sorrow, so that only joy remains.**

The Early Church Was Catholic—
We Should Be Too

The early Church was visible, structured, and apostolic. The modern idea that early Christianity was loose, undefined, or fragmented is a myth. **From the beginning, the Church was visible, hierarchical, and united under apostolic authority.**

In the Book of Acts, we see a clear structure: the apostles lead, teach, and appoint successors. The faithful devote themselves to "the apostles' teaching and to the fellowship, to the breaking of bread and to prayer" (Acts 2:42). This isn't vague spirituality; it's a liturgical, communal, and sacramental life guided **by ordained leaders**.

Paul writes to Timothy and Titus, his appointed bishops, instructing them to govern the Church, appoint presbyters (priests), and safeguard doctrine. This shows the early Church had bishops, priests, and deacons—a threefold ministry still present in the Catholic Church today.

The Church wasn't and isn't just an invisible collection of believers. It had clear boundaries of belief and practice, a sacred liturgy, sacraments, and a living authority.

The Early Church Practiced the Sacraments

From the beginning, Christians practiced baptism, the Eucharist, confession, confirmation, holy orders, marriage, and anointing of the sick.

- Baptism

  - **Acts 2:38**: "Repent and be baptized, every one of you, in the name of Jesus Christ for the forgiveness of your sins."

- ◦ **The Didache** (c. 70 AD) outlines baptismal instructions very similar to Catholic practice.

- Eucharist

  - ◦ The breaking of bread in **Acts 2:42** and Paul's letters (especially 1 Corinthians 10–11) confirm that early Christians believed in the Real Presence of Christ in the Eucharist.

  - ◦ **St. Ignatius of Antioch** (c. 107 AD) wrote: "The Eucharist is the flesh of our Savior Jesus Christ."

- Confession

  - ◦ **James 5:16**: "Confess your sins to one another."

  - ◦ **The Church practiced confession to priests**, as seen in writings from the second century onward:

    - ▪ **The Didache 4:14** "Confess your sins in church, and do not go up to your prayer with an evil conscience." This shows public confession was part of early liturgical life—done in church, within the Christian community.

    - ▪ **St. Irenaeus of Lyons** (c. 180 AD) A disciple of St. Polycarp, who was a disciple of John the Apostle. He recounts how some people confessed their sins to the clergy: "Some of them... confess their sins with great sorrow and penitence, and others—ashamed to do so publicly—withdraw from the hope of God, thinking they cannot obtain pardon." —*Against Heresies, Book I*, Chapter 13. This shows both the expectation of confession and the role of Church authorities in hearing it.

    - ▪ **Tertullian** (c. 203 AD) An early Christian writer from North Africa who confirmed that sacramental confession was practiced: "It is necessary to confess our sins to obtain pardon… The act of confession lightens the burden of our sin."—*On Repentance*, Ch. 10. He also noted that some delayed confession out of pride—meaning it was a known and expected practice.

- **Origen** (c. 244 AD) A famous biblical scholar and Church father: "There is a procedure in the Church, and it is not without reason, that when sinners do penance... they are brought before the bishop or priest and are not ashamed to lay bare their sin."—*Homilies on Leviticus* 2:4. This is a clear reference to confessing sins to a bishop or priest, who had the authority to evaluate and guide the penitent.

- **St. Cyprian of Carthage** (c. 250 AD) Bishop of Carthage, writing during Roman persecution: "Let each confess his sin while he is still in this world... let him make confession to the priests of God."—*The Lapsed*, Ch. 28. (Note: "priests of God"—this wasn't a general "tell your sins to anyone" model. Confession was tied to apostolic authority.)

- **Council of Nicaea** (325 AD) Canon 11 of the council addresses how those who lapsed under persecution must go through confession and penance before being readmitted—under episcopal oversight.

These Sacraments **were not optional symbols but the very means by which grace was given** and the faithful were united to Christ.

The Early Church Worshiped Liturgically

Early Christian worship was **liturgical, structured**, and centered on the **Eucharist**.

St. Justin Martyr (c. 155 AD) described the Mass in striking detail:

> "On the day called Sunday... the memoirs of the apostles or the writings of the prophets are read... Then the president offers prayers... bread and wine and water are brought... and we receive them with thanksgiving, and a distribution is made."

This mirrors the modern Catholic Mass:

- Liturgy of the Word (Scripture readings)

- Prayers of the Faithful

- Offertory and Eucharistic Prayer

- Communion

There is **no mention of solo Bible study, emotional sermons, or entertainment**. Worship was **communal, reverent, sacramental**—and it was Catholic.

The Early Church Believed in Apostolic Succession

The early Christians did not believe each believer could interpret Scripture for themselves. They relied on the teaching of the bishops, who were successors to the apostles.

- **St. Irenaeus** (c. 180 AD), a disciple of St. Polycarp (who was a disciple of St. John), wrote:

  "It is necessary to obey the presbyters who are in the Church—those who have the succession from the apostles..."

The early Church knew that without apostolic teaching authority, **chaos would result**. The Catholic Church today alone maintains that apostolic succession through the laying on of hands has continued unbroken from the apostles to today's bishops.

The Early Church Honored Mary and the Saints

While worship was directed to God alone, early Christians honored Mary and the martyrs, asking for their prayers and celebrating their feast days.

- The earliest known prayer to Mary is from around 250 AD:

  "We fly to your patronage, O holy Mother of God."

Ancient catacomb inscriptions invoke saints. The faithful asked for their intercession just as Catholics do today. Far from being a later invention, the communion of saints was **foundational**.

The Early Church Was Centered in Rome

The bishop of Rome—the Pope—was regarded from the earliest centuries as the successor of Peter and a unique source of unity.

- **St. Ignatius of Antioch** called the Roman Church:

  "The Church which presides in love."

- St. Irenaeus wrote:

  "It is necessary that every Church should agree with [the Roman Church], on account of its preeminent authority."

The Pope's role was not invented in the Middle Ages. There had been thirty-two popes before Emperor Constantine legalized Christianity with the Edict of Milan in 313 AD. From the first centuries, Rome was the **center** of doctrinal unity and appeal.

The Early Church Recognized the Canon of Scripture

The Bible did not fall from the sky. It was the Catholic Church that discerned, compiled, and preserved the canon of Scripture.

- The Councils of Rome (382), Hippo (393), and Carthage (397) set the New Testament canon.

- These councils, guided by the bishops and the Pope, recognized seventy-three inspired books—including the Deuterocanonical books Protestants later removed.

- Without the Catholic Church, there would be no Bible as we know it.

The Early Church Faced Persecution with Courage and Unity

For 300 years, Christianity was illegal. Christians were tortured, imprisoned, and executed—yet the Church did not splinter.

Why? Because the Church was united in faith, liturgy, and hierarchy. The Eucharist was their strength, and the bishops were their shepherds. Martyrs went to their deaths proclaiming loyalty not just to Jesus, but to the Catholic Church, which they called "our mother."

Tertullian (c. 200 AD) famously said:

> "The blood of the martyrs is the seed of the Church."

The Early Church Fathers Were Catholic

Reading the writings of the early Church Fathers reveals clearly Catholic beliefs:

- **St. Clement of Rome** (c. 96 AD): mentions apostolic succession and hierarchy.

- **St. Ignatius of Antioch** (c. 107 AD): teaches the Real Presence in the Eucharist, submission to bishops, and refers to the Church as "Catholic."

- **St. Justin Martyr** (c. 155 AD): describes the Mass and defends the Eucharist.

- **St. Irenaeus** (c. 180 AD): defends apostolic tradition and the authority of Rome.

None of them taught "Bible alone" or "faith alone." All of them sound Catholic, not Protestant.

Why We Should Be Catholic Too

If the early Church was Catholic, then to be **fully Christian** is to be Catholic.

Today, many Christians love Jesus and Scripture but have unknowingly inherited a *partial version* of Christianity, **separated from the fullness of the faith**:

- Without the Eucharist

- Without apostolic authority

- Without Mary and the saints

- Without the sacramental life

Conclusion: Imitations Fade–The True Church Remains

To come home to the Catholic Church is not to abandon your love for Jesus—it is to embrace everything He gave us. The early Church was a **visible, unified, and sacramental community, centered on the teachings of the apostles and the breaking of the bread—the Eucharist.** It had a clear structure with bishops, priests, and deacons, led by the apostles and their successors through apostolic succession. **Worship was liturgical,** not casual or entertainment-based, and focused on prayer, Scripture, and the Eucharist, as described in Acts 2:42.

The early Christians believed in the Real Presence of Christ in the Eucharist, practiced baptism for the forgiveness of sins, and upheld Sacred Tradition along with Scripture. They honored Mary and the saints, asked for their intercession, and looked to the bishop of Rome as a source of unity and authority. Despite intense persecution, the Church remains steadfast, unified in faith, doctrine, and sacramental life—clearly Catholic in belief and practice from the very beginning. The lack of authority in Protestantism led to fragmentation and a drift away from Christ-centered worship.

"The Catholic Church is not only the true Church, she is also my true home. I did not lose anything in becoming Catholic—I gained the fullness of Christ."

—Dr. Peter Kreeft (former Calvinist)

Anti-Catholicism in America: Mistaking Rebellion for Freedom Since 1776

I love America. I'm deeply grateful to live in this country, but as a Catholic living in Oklahoma who has lived in and visited numerous states through the Midwest and South, I personally have experienced a deep fear and hatred born out of ignorance for the Catholic Church.

In the earliest days of Christianity, to be Christian was to be Catholic. And that is still true in much of the world today. It's not even controversial. **It's simply the normal understanding of Christianity: ancient, historical, and consistent**. From Europe to South America, Africa to Asia, Catholicism remains the largest Christian body by far, recognized as the Church founded by Christ Himself.

So why is it so different in America?

Here, Catholicism is often seen as strange, suspect, even un-Christian. Protestants—who inherited a deep distrust of Catholicism from their European forefathers—arrived on American soil determined to escape anything they perceived as "Old World" control: monarchy, hierarchy, and, yes, the authority of the Church. Rebellion was baked into the American identity from the beginning—political rebellion, religious rebellion, personal rebellion. **Hyper-independence** became a cultural virtue. **Authority** became the enemy.

In this environment, the Catholic Church—a visible, structured, hierarchical Church founded by Christ and sustained by the authority He gave to the apostles—seemed incompatible with the American spirit. It smelled too much like monarchy, too much like rules, too much like someone telling them what to do or believe.

And yet, Catholicism isn't about domination. It's about truth, which encompasses freedom.

It is the family God established to safeguard His teachings, Sacraments, and saving grace.

The authority of the Church is not human tyranny; it's the loving order and guardrails of a Father who wants His children to thrive in unity and truth. Authority doesn't crush freedom; it **protects it from the chaos of self-made religions and endless divisions.**

Authority, Rightly Ordered, Is Not a Cage—It's a Guardrail for Freedom.

Many Americans have grown up with a political lens so firmly attached to their spiritual vision that **they struggle to recognize true Christianity when they see it.** Anything that looks structured, compassionate, or merciful is instantly suspected of being "leftist," "soft," or "compromised."

Satan has cleverly inverted true compassion by counterfeiting it through secular ideologies, making it even harder for wounded, hyper-independent hearts to recognize **real mercy** when God offers it.

This rebellion—emotional as much as intellectual—blinds many to the beauty of the Church, just as it blinds them to good and holy leaders within her. Few examples illustrate this better than the way many Americans misunderstood and vilified Pope Francis.

When I entered the Church, I did so carrying much of this rebellion. I clung to my pride and self-reliance even as I claimed to embrace Christ's Church. Like many, I judged Pope Francis through media headlines, the voices of popular influencers, and political commentators, rather than through **his own words and actions.**

It wasn't until I humbled myself, unfollowed the dissident voices, and

read his writings for myself that I saw the truth: **a shepherd profoundly attuned to the heart of Christ—merciful, compassionate, and unwavering in truth**.

If Jesus Himself stood before us today, would we recognize Him? Or would we dismiss Him too—for offering mercy instead of political dominance?

Americans, especially, seem to struggle with receiving God's mercy because we have been taught to view authority as oppression and compassion as weakness.

Unfortunately, most Americans who reject Catholicism don't really know what they're rejecting.

They know a caricature, not the reality.

They see Catholicism as dead religion—"rituals," "works-based salvation," or "Mary worship"—none of which are true. They believe the Church invented traditions to control people, rather than receiving and **guarding the deposit of faith entrusted by Christ** (2 Timothy 1:13–14).

But it must also be said: distrust of Catholicism in America has not been fueled only by ignorance.

Some of it has been **deliberately manufactured by powerful forces**.

Political leaders, cultural elites, and major media outlets have long seen the Catholic Church as a threat—not because it was corrupt but **because it stood firm against moral relativism**, secularism, and political control. A Church that teaches objective truth, absolute moral standards, and **loyalty to Christ above the state** is a serious obstacle to any agenda based on power, profit, or ideology. As a result, Catholicism has been systematically attacked, distorted, and vilified in the American cultural imagination.

As Venerable Archbishop Fulton J. Sheen wisely said:

"There are not one hundred people in the United States who hate the Catholic Church. There are millions, however, who hate what they wrongly believe the Catholic Church to be."

Rather than seeing the Church as a **guardian of truth and freedom**, many Americans have been taught, often unconsciously, to view it as oppressive, outdated, or dangerous. And so, even without fully understanding what they are rejecting, many Americans have learned to distrust the Catholic Church almost by instinct. But judging the Church by the narratives of her enemies is no different than judging Jesus by the accusations of His persecutors. **The divine institution remains holy, even when the world wages war against it.**

As Christians, we have a duty to "study to show ourselves approved" (2 Timothy 2:15)—to seek truth with humility, to learn the real history and teachings of our faith.

If we are willing to lay down our pride and ask hard questions— about history, about the Bible, about the early Church—God will reveal the truth. And when we finally see it, the truth becomes impossible to ignore.

A History of Hostility

Anti-Catholicism is not a modern invention; it's one of the oldest prejudices woven into America's history. **From the earliest colonial days, Catholics were viewed with suspicion and hostility**. In several English colonies, including Massachusetts and New York, **Catholic Mass was illegal. Priests risked imprisonment or exile** simply for ministering to the faithful (Noll, *The Old Religion in a New World*). Even Maryland, originally founded as a refuge for Catholics fleeing persecution in England, eventually bowed to Protestant pressure and **passed laws**

barring Catholics from voting, holding office, or openly practicing their faith (Massa, *Anti-Catholicism in America*).

By the nineteenth century, anti-Catholicism had become an open political movement.

The **Know-Nothing Party**, active in the 1840s and 1850s, rose to power by **spreading lies** that Catholics were plotting to overthrow American democracy at the Pope's command (Billington, *The Protestant Crusade*). Mobs, driven by fear and hatred, burned Catholic churches and convents, as seen in the **Ursuline Convent riots of 1834** in Charlestown, Massachusetts (Miller, *City of the Century*).

The hatred persisted into the twentieth century. In the 1920s, the **Ku Klux Klan** expanded its targets to **include Catholics alongside Black Americans and Jews**, burning crosses outside Catholic churches and violently opposing Catholic education (Chalmers, *Hooded Americanism*). States like Oregon even **passed laws attempting to forcibly close Catholic schools** through the Compulsory Education Act of 1922, a measure supported by the KKK. It was overturned only by the Supreme Court in *Pierce v. Society of Sisters* (1925), a landmark decision defending religious liberty (Green, *The Bible, the School, and the Constitution*).

Even presidential **politics were not immune to anti-Catholic bigotry.** In 1928, **Al Smith**, the first Catholic nominee for president, lost in a landslide largely because of widespread fear that he would take orders from the Vatican (Allitt, *Catholic Converts*). In 1960, **John F. Kennedy** was forced to publicly assure Protestant voters that his loyalty was to the Constitution, not the Pope (Cogley, *Religion in the Presidential Campaign*).

While open discrimination has faded from law, it has never fully disappeared from the culture.

Today, **mainstream media frequently misrepresents Catholic**

teaching, especially on moral issues like marriage, abortion, and religious freedom (Weigel, *The Irony of Modern Catholic History*).

Scandals involving individual Catholics are portrayed as systemic failures of the Church itself, even though statistically, abuse rates are lower in Catholic institutions than in comparable secular settings (Jenkins, *Pedophiles and Priests*).

Throughout American history, Catholics have not been treated as defenders of freedom, but as threats to it, a bitter irony considering that **the Catholic Church is the original guardian of the moral truths that make true freedom possible.**

Conclusion: Removing the Political Scales from Our Eyes

For most of the world, **Catholicism simply is Christianity**. It's not "one option among many." It's the faith Christ gave to the world, preserved across centuries—not by human achievement, but by divine providence.

America's instinct to rebel against authority may be understandable. But when it leads us **to rebel against the authority of Christ Himself, working through His Church**, it costs us more than political loyalty. It costs us the fullness of the truth. **And it can cost us our soul.**

The Catholic Church is not a political movement. It is not a medieval invention created by Constantine. It is the living, breathing family of God, entrusted with truth, mercy, and the healing of wounded hearts.

To truly see the Church—and to see good and holy leaders like Pope Francis rightly—we must put down our political weapons, remove the filters of suspicion and pride, and allow Christ to open our eyes. **Only humility can heal the blindness rebellion has caused.**

It is not the Church that has failed America. It is America that has failed to recognize the Church—standing as a light in the darkness, even while the world tries to extinguish it.

The Catholic Church endures not because of human strength, but because of divine protection. She is not the enemy of freedom, but its surest defender. She is not the oppressor of souls, but their true home.

For those willing to receive her, the Catholic Church offers something this world cannot give:

the **fullness of truth**, the balm of mercy, and the enduring promise of Christ Himself.

"He who listens to you listens to Me" (Luke 10:16).

What Aboutism:
The Church Scandal

This is a difficult but important topic. We want to be thoughtful and faithful in our response, to uphold the truth of the Church while acknowledging its failures and the pain caused to victims.

The sexual abuse scandal in the Catholic Church is a tragic and painful chapter in modern Church history. **There is no excuse for the sins committed by some members of the clergy,** nor for the failure of some leaders to respond swiftly and justly. These acts brought deep harm to victims and immense scandal to the faithful. As Catholics, we mourn with the victims, pray for their healing, and support every effort toward justice and accountability.

As we keep that in mind, it is crucial to distinguish between the sinfulness of individuals and the holiness of the Church as the Body of Christ. **Jesus Himself warned that there would be weeds among the wheat** (Matthew 13:24–30), and He chose twelve apostles, knowing that **one would betray Him**. The Church, being **both human and divine,** carries the treasure of Christ's truth in earthen vessels (2 Corinthians 4:7). But despite the failings of her members, **the Church cannot teach error in faith or morals, because she is guided and protected by the Holy Spirit** (John 16:13). **Her divine foundation remains firm:** "You are Peter, and on this rock I will build my Church, and the gates of hell shall not prevail against it" (Matthew 16:18).

In response to the crisis, the Catholic Church has made substantial reforms. In fact, studies now show that the Church is one of the **safest institutions** for children and vulnerable adults today. Policies like zero-tolerance, mandatory background checks, safe environment train-ing, and external reporting procedures have been put in place around the world, especially in the United States. The Church has worked hard to remove abusive clergy, prevent future abuse, and foster a culture of accountability and transparency.

The scandal does not disprove the Church's divine origin—it proves that we need grace, holiness, and the Sacraments more than ever. The Church is not holy because all her members are saints; she is holy because she is the Bride of Christ, entrusted with the fullness of truth and grace. We stay not because her members are perfect, but because **Christ is perfect, and He remains present in His Church, especially in the Eucharist**.

While even one case of abuse is too many, let's review the broader data to help clarify how the Catholic Church compares to other insti-tutions—including schools, families, and other religious groups—and shows how the Church has taken extraordinary steps to become one of the safest environments today.

Contextual Statistics on Sexual Abuse

General Statistics on Abuse (U.S.):

Most abuse occurs in the home. Over 80% of sexual abuse cases are committed by family members or someone known to the child (U.S. Dept. of Justice). Statistics consistently show that **the highest perpe-trators of sexual abuse against children are not clergy, teachers, or strangers—but people within the home**, especially **biological fathers, stepfathers, and the mother's boyfriend**. Here are some key facts:

The U.S. Department of Justice and National Center for Victims of Crime report that:

- **Family members** commit 30–40% of child sexual abuse.

- The mother's **boyfriend or stepfather is one of the most common** abusers in non-stranger abuse cases.

According to a study published in *Child Abuse & Neglect*:

- Children are **5 to 10 times more likely** to be abused by someone they know and live with than by strangers or authority figures outside the home.

The National Sexual Violence Resource Center confirms:

- **93% of child sexual abuse victims know their abuser.**

- The **largest percentage** involves a parent, step-parent, or other relative.

Factually speaking, **fathers, stepfathers, and male partners of mothers are statistically the most frequent perpetrators** of sexual abuse against children—not Catholic priests, not clergy, and certainly not "the Church" as a whole. That doesn't excuse abuse in any institution, but it **absolutely destroys the myth** that the Catholic Church is somehow the epicenter of the problem. The harsh truth is that the greatest danger to a child is usually much closer to home.

- **Public Schools**:

  According to a U.S. Department of Education report (Charol Shakeshaft, 2004), an estimated 9.6% of public school students report educator sexual misconduct—that's 1 in 10 students.

- **Catholic Church**:

  The John Jay Report (commissioned by the U.S. bishops, 2004) found that:

  - **Approximately 4% of priests** between 1950–2002 were accused of abuse.

- The annual rate of new cases **dropped dramatically** after 1985 and continues to remain extremely low.

- The majority of reported abuse cases occurred between the 1960s and 1980s, with a peak in the 1970s—long before most of the Church's reforms were put in place.

- Since the early 2000s, the Church has had one of the **lowest abuse rates** among major institutions.

How the Catholic Church Compares Today

The Catholic Church:

- Extensive safeguarding protocols, including:
    - Mandatory background checks
    - Zero-tolerance policies
    - Safe Environment training
    - Mandatory reporting to civil authorities
    - Lay oversight boards
- According to multiple studies, including work by The Center for Applied Research in the Apostolate:
    - **New credible allegations are rare, especially among newly ordained priests.**
    - **The Church today is among the lowest-risk environments for children.**

Other Institutions:

- **Public school systems have far higher rates of misconduct**, often underreported or handled quietly.

- Other religious denominations have also faced abuse scandals, but without the same level of media scrutiny or institutional reform.

- Youth organizations, sports teams, and even the medical field have all experienced high-profile abuse cases, yet they receive **far less sustained criticism** than the Church.

Abuse Rates: Catholic vs. Protestant Churches

Catholic Church

- The **John Jay Report** (2004), commissioned by the U.S. Conference of Catholic Bishops, found that:

    ○ **4% of priests** active between 1950 and 2002 had been accused of sexual abuse of minors.

    ○ Abuse cases peaked between the 1960s and the 1980s.

    ○ Over **80%** of victims were **male**, often adolescent boys (ages 11–17).

- Since 2002, the Catholic Church in the U.S. has implemented rigorous **safeguards**, making it **one of the most compliant institutions** in terms of child protection protocols.

Protestant Churches

- Protestant denominations, being numerous and decentralized, **do not maintain a centralized reporting system like the Catholic Church**, which makes national-level data difficult to compile.

- However, a 2007 Associated Press investigation reported that **Protestant clergy were accused of sexual misconduct more often than Catholic clergy** in the U.S. Based on insurance claims and denominational records, the data showed an average of 260

Protestant clergy accused per year, compared to 228 Catholic clergy at the height of the abuse crisis.

- In addition, a **2002 report from Christian Ministry Resources**—a Protestant legal and risk management organization—found that among churches reporting abuse cases, **Protestant churches outnumbered Catholic churches by a ratio of 3 to 1.**

According to **Dr. Philip Jenkins**, a non-Catholic historian and expert on religion and abuse:

"We have no evidence that Catholic clergy are more likely to abuse than other clergy or, indeed, than non-clerical professionals working with children." *("Pedophiles and Priests," 2001)*

Conclusion: Truth and Justice Together

The Catholic Church is both human and divine and does not deny or excuse past failures. Instead, it has acknowledged them, repented, and reformed. In doing so, it has become a global model for child protection. While pain and scandal remain, it's important to judge the Church by her teachings and reforms, not just the personal failures of some members.

While both Catholic and Protestant churches have faced serious and tragic abuse cases, the data shows that abuse is **not uniquely a Catholic problem**. In fact, multiple independent studies have shown that abuse allegations are statistically *higher* among Protestant clergy, public school employees, and even family members—yet the Catholic Church has become the cultural scapegoat precisely because it holds itself to a higher moral standard and maintains centralized accountability.

Regardless of denomination, **every church bears the responsibility to protect the vulnerable** and ensure leadership is held accountable.

The media often highlights the Catholic Church disproportionately, but

facts show that when it comes to abuse prevention and response, the **Catholic Church is now one of the safest institutions** in the world. The abuse scandal within the Catholic Church is a horrific wound—one that cannot be minimized, excused, or brushed aside. It has caused incalculable pain, driven souls from the faith, and cast a long shadow over the witness of the Gospel. Those wounds deserve justice. **Survivors deserve to be heard and protected**. And the Church must continue to repent, reform, and remain vigilant in rooting out evil wherever it hides.

But acknowledging the gravity of this scandal does not mean we abandon truth or lose perspective. **Abuse is not unique to the Catholic Church**—it is a devastating epidemic across all institutions: schools, sports teams, families, Protestant churches, and secular organizations.

That doesn't mean we deflect or minimize what happened. **It means we face the truth fully**—without distortion, without deflection, and without abandoning the very Church Christ founded. In the words of Pope Benedict XVI, "We are not looking for a Church that pleases us... but for the Church that is true." If the Catholic Church is the true Church, then even amid scandal, we do not walk away—we stay, we purify, and we help her become more radiant through reform and holiness.

Scandal is real—but so is redemption. And the Church is not a museum of saints. It is a hospital for sinners, including her clergy. The worst response is to sever ourselves from the very graces—the Eucharist, the sacraments, the authority of truth—that can heal us and restore what evil tried to destroy.

Hold your leaders accountable. Never tolerate abuse. But don't let the sins of men drive you from the Bride of Christ. She is still holy, not because her members always are, but because Christ Himself is holy—and He promised the gates of hell would not prevail.

Religion or Relationship— Why Not Both?

"Christianity is a relationship, not a religion."

It's a phrase you'll hear often in Protestant circles, usually meant to emphasize the deeply personal nature of faith—that following Jesus is about knowing Him, not just following rules. And in that sense, it's absolutely right. But it's also a **false dichotomy**. It suggests that religion and relationship are somehow at odds, as if structure, doctrine, and sacramental life hinder intimacy with God. In Catholicism, nothing could be further from the truth. It's not **religion versus relationship**—it's **both**, beautifully woven together by God's design.

Jesus didn't come simply to inspire or to hand down a new moral code. He came to **unite us to Himself**—in mind, in heart, and even in body. That's why He established the Church, not as an optional institution, but as His **mystical Body on earth**. That's why He gave us the Sacraments, not as empty rituals, but as living encounters with grace—real, tangible ways to receive His divine life. In the Catholic Church, relationship with Jesus is not reduced to emotion or intellect. It's sacramental. It's incarnational. It's as intimate as receiving His very Body and Blood into your own.

The structure, liturgy, and teachings of the Church aren't barriers to relationship with God—they're the framework through which that relationship is nurtured and sustained. Like the guardrails on a bridge, Catholicism offers both direction and safety as we journey toward Christ. The earliest Christians understood this. **Acts 2:42** shows how the first believers lived:

"They devoted themselves to the apostles' teaching and fellowship, to the breaking of bread and the prayers."

That's **doctrine, sacrament, and community**—the same elements still present in the Church today.

The New Testament never pits relationship against religion. In fact, **James 1:27** says:

"Religion that is pure and undefiled before God the Father is this: to visit orphans and widows in their affliction, and to keep oneself unstained from the world."

Religion isn't the enemy. Hypocrisy is.

This harmony between faith and structure is confirmed in the early Church. **St. Ignatius of Antioch**, writing in AD 107, urged Christians to remain united with their bishop, celebrate one Eucharist, and **avoid division**. He didn't describe Christianity as a "just me and my Bible alone" personal journey detached from community or sacraments—he called the Eucharist *"the medicine of immortality,"* and insisted that unity with the Church was unity with Christ.

The modern tendency to reject "organized religion" is often rooted in pain, mistrust, or modern individualism. It's used to justify spiritual minimalism: "I don't need the Church—I have Jesus." But following Jesus **always meant following Him into His Church**. He said, *"He who hears you, hears Me"* (*Luke 10:16*) and *"Upon this rock I will build My Church"* (*Matthew 16:18*). He promised to be with it always (*Matthew 28:20*) and to guide it into all truth (*John 16:13*). The Church is not a man-made barrier to Christ. It's His **gift to us**—the vessel of His presence, His authority, and His grace.

Catholicism doesn't reduce the Christian life to **cold ritual** or **emotionalism**. It sees the fullness:

- **Scripture and Tradition** (*2 Thessalonians 2:15*)

- **Faith and works** (*James 2:24*)

- **Grace and cooperation** (*Philippians 2:12–13*)

- **Personal relationship and communal worship** (*Hebrews 10:25*)

This is not contradiction—it's synergy. Not confusion—but clarity. The Church doesn't ask you to choose between truth and love, spirit and structure, or doctrine and devotion. It invites you to live fully in the **both/and** mystery of faith.

Through the Sacraments, Catholics don't just talk about Jesus. We **encounter** Him:

- In **Baptism**, we are spiritually reborn into His Body.

- In **Confession**, we hear His words of mercy spoken aloud through the priest: *"I absolve you."*

- In the **Eucharist**, we receive Jesus—not symbolically, but really, truly, and substantially. Body, Blood, Soul, and Divinity.

- In **Confirmation**, the Holy Spirit seals us with His gifts.

- In **Marriage** and **Holy Orders**, Christ binds people in sacred covenant and pours out grace for their lifelong vocations.

- In the **Anointing of the Sick**, Christ brings healing and strength to those suffering.

Every sacrament is a personal, physical, and spiritual touchpoint with Jesus Christ. They are not just rituals—they are **encounters with the living God**.

This is the ultimate relationship: to be united to Christ not just emotionally or intellectually, but **sacramentally and spiritually**—fully, completely, and bodily. When someone says, *"I don't want religion, I want relationship,"* a Catholic can joyfully respond:

"Then come to the Eucharist—because there's no closer relationship than being united to Jesus Christ in His very flesh and blood."

The Catholic Church doesn't oppose relationship—it **perfects it** through the grace and truth of Christ, offered to us in love, through the Church He founded. The idea of "religion vs. relationship" is often used to contrast **empty rule-following** with genuine connection to God. But in reality, **true religion** and **authentic relationship** go hand in hand.

Jesus Was Religious

It's become fashionable in some circles to claim that Jesus opposed religion—as if He came to dismantle ritual, doctrine, or structure in favor of pure personal experience. But that's a false narrative rooted more in modern discomfort with authority than in biblical truth. **Jesus was not anti-religious. He was deeply religious.** As a faithful Jew living in the time of the Second Temple, He observed the Law, honored the liturgical calendar, participated in temple worship, and upheld the sacrificial system—all without apology or contradiction. Far from rejecting religion, Jesus **fulfilled it** (Matthew 5:17), grounding His mission not in rebellion against tradition, but in its divine completion.

Jesus was circumcised on the eighth day (Luke 2:21). He was presented in the Temple, in accordance with Jewish law (Luke 2:22–24). As a boy, He was found teaching in the Temple during Passover (Luke 2:41–49). He read from the scroll in synagogue (Luke 4:16–20). He kept the Sabbath. He observed ritual feasts like **Passover** (Luke 22:8), **Tabernacles** (John 7:2,10), and **Hanukkah** (John 10:22–23). He paid the Temple tax (Matthew 17:24–27). He even instructed people whom He healed to go show themselves to the priests and make the prescribed offering (Luke 5:14)—in obedience to Levitical law.

Jesus didn't mock religion. He fulfilled it (Matthew 5:17).

What Jesus **did** condemn was empty ritualism—religion without relationship, form without faith, lips that honored God while hearts remained far from Him (Matthew 15:8–9). But that's not a rebuke of religion itself—it's a rebuke of hypocrisy. You don't tear down the house because some people track in mud.

Jesus clearly **respected structure, hierarchy, and sacramental signs**. He preached in synagogues. He taught with authority. He appointed Twelve apostles—a clear parallel to the twelve tribes of Israel. He gave them power to forgive sins (John 20:23), to bind and loose (Matthew 18:18), to break bread in remembrance of Him (Luke 22:19). He didn't say "run wild." He said "go and make disciples… teaching them to observe all that I commanded you" (Matthew 28:19–20).

The entire framework of the Church—its liturgy, sacraments, hierarchy—isn't a man-made invention. It's **divine continuity** with what Jesus practiced and fulfilled.

This modern dichotomy between religion and relationship is not only historically dishonest—it's spiritually lazy. It gives people permission to **reject discipline, ignore authority, and reinvent Christianity around their preferences**. But true religion—rightly ordered worship, doctrine, and devotion—is precisely what safeguards relationship with Christ from being swallowed up by emotion, error, or personal whim.

Contrary to the popular claim that "Jesus came to abolish religion," Scripture actually affirms the structure, authority, and sacrificial worship that **define true religion**. James 1:27 tells us plainly that *"religion that is pure and undefiled before God"* involves both moral action and personal holiness—not empty ritual, but **rightly ordered devotion**. From the very beginning, the early Church was anything but formless. Acts 2:42 shows believers devoted to *"the apostles' teaching, the breaking of bread, and the prayers"*—a clear reference to **structured liturgical worship**.

Jesus Himself **did not abolish the religious system** of the Old Covenant; He fulfilled it (Matthew 5:17), and in doing so, He instituted something even greater. At the Last Supper, He commanded, *"Do this in remembrance of Me"* (Luke 22:19)—establishing a sacramental act, not an emotional abstraction. Hebrews 13:10 even speaks of a Christian *altar*—a bold affirmation that the New Covenant includes real sacrifice, not just praise. **And it is the Church, not individual opinion**, that Paul calls *"the pillar and bulwark of truth"* (1 Timothy 3:15**). Christianity has never been about rejecting religion**—it has always been about living it rightly, in spirit and in truth, under the authority of Christ and the Church He established. **Jesus was religious.** And in following Him, so are we.

Conclusion: Relationship Fulfilled Through Religion

I hope you can see it's not one or the other. It's relationship through religion. It's intimacy through structure. It's grace through the Church. **Because Jesus didn't come to cancel religion**—He came to **fulfill it** (*Matthew 5:17*). And through the Church He established, He still offers us the fullness of that relationship today. Jesus didn't want to abolish religion—He perfected it. He didn't come to erase structure, ritual, or sacred tradition; He came to embody them, fulfill them, and transfigure them into means of grace. The Catholic Church preserves that same incarnational logic: **sacraments instead of sentiment, structure instead of spiritual vagueness, and a relationship with God that is not just emotional, but sacramental and real.**

In the end, it was never religion *versus* relationship. True religion is what anchors, protects, and expresses authentic relationship with Christ. **A faith without form drifts into abstraction.** A relationship without structure becomes sentimentality. But a relationship expressed through right worship, sacramental grace, and obedience to Christ through His Church—that's the faith Jesus practiced, preached, and passed on.

Chosen, Not Silenced:
The Truth About Women and The
Catholic Church

When critics claim that the Catholic Church is oppressive to women, they reveal a stunning ignorance of both history and reality. Far from repressing women, the Catholic Church has **consistently elevated their dignity, championed their unique role in salvation history, and given them a place of honor unmatched by any secular movement.**

In fact, from the very beginning, Catholicism has recognized women not as second-class citizens but as vital participants in God's divine plan.

Mary: The Crown of Creation

At the very center of Catholic theology stands a woman: Mary, the Mother of God. No mere afterthought, no incidental figure, Mary is called **the Queen of Heaven** (Revelation 12:1) and venerated as the New Eve, whose "yes" to God reversed the tragedy unleashed by the first Eve's disobedience.

The Church's profound reverence for Mary is not a sideline devotion— it is a theological statement about the dignity, strength, and unique cooperation of women in the work of salvation. **Mary shows that femininity is not a weakness to be "overcome" but a divine gift to be celebrated.**

No secular institution or feminist movement has ever placed a woman in so exalted a position as the Catholic Church has placed Mary.

Doctors of the Church: Women's Intellectual Might

The title "Doctor of the Church" is one of the **highest honors** in Catholicism, reserved for those whose teachings have had an extraordinary impact on the faith. Of the thirty-seven Doctors of the Church, **four are women**—and all were given this title precisely because of their *intellectual brilliance* and *spiritual authority.*

At a time when most of the world denied women any intellectual standing, the Catholic Church publicly proclaimed women as its greatest teachers.

Women Saints: Models of Holiness and Power

Throughout history, the Catholic Church has recognized countless women not just as faithful followers but as **spiritual giants**—many of whom became the **greatest saints and leaders** in Church history.

Some of the most beloved and influential saints are women:

- **St. Therese of Lisieux** ("The Little Flower")–Declared a Doctor of the Church for her profound teachings on spiritual childhood and trust in God.

- **St. Catherine of Siena**–A laywoman and Doctor of the Church who boldly advised popes and helped end the Avignon Papacy.

- **St. Teresa of Ávila**–(My confirmation saint!) A mystic reformer of the Carmelite order, and Doctor of the Church, whose writings on contemplative prayer remain spiritual masterpieces.

- **St. Hildegard of Bingen**–A twelfth-century polymath: abbess, scientist, physician, composer, theologian, and mystic, also named Doctor of the Church.

- **St. Joan of Arc**–A teenage girl who led armies, counseled kings, and ultimately laid down her life in defense of God's call.

These women were not hidden away or silenced. They were embraced, canonized, and held up for all the world to see.

Jesus Himself shattered the cultural norms of His time regarding women. In a world where women were often dismissed, invisible in court, and marginalized in public life, **Jesus spoke openly with women, healed them, praised their faith, and entrusted them with critical missions**. It was a woman—Mary—who brought Christ into the world. It was women who remained with Him at the foot of the Cross when almost all the apostles had fled. And it was women—**not men**—who were the first witnesses to the Resurrection, the greatest event in human history. Far from sidelining women, **Jesus elevated them to a place of honor**, making them essential witnesses to the Gospel from the very beginning.

The Church vs. the Secular World

Far from oppressing women, the Catholic Church **has liberated them**, in direct contradiction to the culture of the ancient world, where women were often treated as property, had little legal standing, and were excluded from public life.

- The Church taught the equal dignity of women and men, both made in the image of God (Genesis 1:27).

- The Church insisted on the indissolubility of the sacrament of marriage, protecting women from abandonment and exploitation.

- The Church condemned abortion and infanticide, common practices in ancient pagan societies that disproportionately harmed women and female infants.

- Religious orders offered women leadership opportunities, education, and autonomy centuries before secular institutions even considered the idea.

It was often the Catholic nuns, not secular governments, who built the first hospitals, schools, and universities for girls and women.

Why Only Men Can Be Priests—and Why It's Not an Insult to Women

One of the most common misunderstandings today is the claim that the Catholic Church is "sexist" because it reserves the priesthood to men. But this objection misunderstands both the nature of the priesthood and the profound dignity of women.

The Catholic priest is not simply a "leader" or "organizer" of the community, like a modern corporate manager. The priest stands *in persona Christi*—**in the person of Christ**—during the Sacraments, especially at the altar during the Holy Sacrifice of the Mass. **He is a visible, sacramental sign of Jesus Christ, the Bridegroom, offering Himself for His Bride, the Church.**

Because Jesus Himself—God Incarnate—chose to come into the world as a man and instituted only men as His apostles, **the Church remains faithful to His design**, not because men are "better," but because the priest must **sacramentally** represent Christ the Bridegroom. It is a matter of divine symbolism and faithfulness, not personal worth.

Far from diminishing women, this reality actually **preserves the dignity of both vocations**—masculine and feminine—as **complementary and vital** to the life of the Church. Women are called to a full and profound participation in the life of the Church, and history shows they have excelled as saints, theologians, mystics, missionaries, teachers, abbesses, and leaders of Catholic civilization. **But the priesthood is a particular sacramental role, just as motherhood is a particular sacramental role**, and denying this difference would flatten and distort the beauty of God's plan.

As Pope St. John Paul II definitively stated in *Ordinatio Sacerdotalis*

(1994), *"The Church has no authority whatsoever to confer priestly ordination on women, and this judgment is to be definitively held by all the Church's faithful."*

In other words, it's not a rule the Church could simply change even if she wanted to. It is rooted in the very nature of Christ's plan—and fidelity to His example is the Church's glory, not her shame.

The greatest woman who ever lived—the Blessed Virgin Mary—was not a priest. And yet no man, priest or Pope, will ever surpass her holiness, her dignity, or her closeness to God. The greatness of women in the Church **does not come from imitation of men** but from living the full splendor of womanhood that God designed.

Conclusion: The True Liberator of Women

From the very beginning, the Church has recognized the **profound dignity and mission of women**. It is no coincidence that at the center of Catholic devotion stands a woman: Mary, the Queen of Heaven. **It is no accident** that the first witnesses to the Resurrection were women, honored by Christ Himself. And it is no accident that some of the Church's greatest saints, mystics, doctors, and martyrs are women whose influence shaped Christianity and Western civilization itself.

Even the reservation of the priesthood to men is not a slight against women but a fidelity to Christ's will and the deeper sacramental meaning of the Church. Just as Christ the Bridegroom is represented by the male priest, **so too does the feminine genius of the Church—** the Bride—shine forth most perfectly in the holiness and strength of women. The Catholic Church does not pit men and women against each other in competition but celebrates their God-given differences and **complementary missions**.

Far from being an oppressor of women, the Catholic Church has always been—and remains—their greatest champion. Where the world offers a counterfeit empowerment based on competition and sameness, the Church offers **true liberation grounded in love, dignity, and eternal purpose.**

Because it's not the world that crowned a woman Queen of Heaven—it's Christ Himself.

The Catholic Church vs. The Crafty Counterfeit

As a former Luciferian, let me be clear: Accusing the Catholic Church of witchcraft is not only **absurd**, it reveals a profound ignorance of both Catholicism and spiritual reality.

Witchcraft and the occult are not reflections of the Catholic faith. They are satanic *counterfeits*—inversions of what Christ gave us through His Church. Satan doesn't create. He *can't*. He is a creation; therefore, he can only twist, counterfeit, and corrupt what God has made.

The Catholic Church: Eternal in Christ

Many people mistakenly believe the Catholic Church is just a human institution that started centuries after Christ. But Scripture tells a different story.

The Church is not merely a human invention—it was present *in the mind of God from the beginning of time*:

- **Ephesians 1:4–5:**

  "He chose us in Him, before the foundation of the world, to be holy and blameless before Him. In love He destined us for adoption to Himself through Jesus Christ."

- **Ephesians 3:10–11:**

  "So that through the Church the manifold wisdom of God might now be made known... according to the eternal purpose that He accomplished in Christ Jesus our Lord."

The Church isn't *Plan B*. It was God's eternal design to unite heaven and earth **through Christ and His Bride—the Church** (see **Revelation 21:2**).

When Jesus said to Peter in **Matthew 16:18**, "You are Peter, and upon this rock I will build my Church, and the gates of hell shall not prevail against it," He was not founding a mere denomination. He was establishing an indestructible, divine reality that already existed in the heart of the Father.

Thus, the Catholic Church in her **divine essence** is timeless—rooted in Christ Himself, extending into eternity.

Sacramentals: God's Instruments, Not Pagan Superstition

From the beginning, the Church has used **sacramentals**—physical matter blessed by the Church to prepare us to receive grace. Sacramentals are *not* magic. **They are not attempts to control God or the spiritual world**. They are tangible reminders that God, who became incarnate (John 1:14), still works through material reality to reach and sanctify us. Examples of sacramentals from the earliest Church include:

- **Blessed water:** Foreshadowed in Jewish purification rites; fulfilled in Christian baptismal waters (**John 3:5**).

- **Incense:** Used in the Jewish Temple (**Exodus 30:34–38**) and carried into Christian worship (**Revelation 8:3–4**).

- **Blessed oil:** Used for anointing (**Mark 6:13**) and codified in the Sacraments of the Church.

- **Holy relics:** The early Christians preserved the remains of martyrs, believing them to be sources of intercession and blessing (see **2 Kings 13:21**, where a dead man revived after touching Elisha's bones).

From the beginning, the early Christians understood that **matter itself could be sanctified by God**.

God created the material world and called it "very good" (Genesis 1:31). The Incarnation proved forever that God *uses* **the physical to bring about the spiritual**. Far from being "pagan," sacramentals are **biblically rooted**, part of the Church's original worship, and were always understood as **pointing to Christ**, not replacing Him.

The "New Age" Is Just Old Paganism

Despite its trendy name, the New Age movement is nothing new. It is simply a *recycling* of ancient pagan ideas with fresh branding.

- **Crystal healing, astrology, manifestation rituals**, and **spirit channeling** all trace their roots to practices condemned by God in the Old Testament (Deuteronomy 18:10–12).

- **Saging** and **energy cleansing** are modern spins on ancient superstitions that the early Christians rejected in favor of Christ's victory over sin and death.

- **"Manifesting your desires"** is simply a repackaging of sorcery—the attempt to manipulate spiritual forces for personal gain.

Ecclesiastes 1:9 says it plainly: "There is nothing new under the sun." **The "New Age" isn't new**. It's simply rebellion in a new outfit. Meanwhile, the Catholic Church—often accused of being "pagan" by those who don't understand her—**has *always* opposed the occult, witchcraft, and false spiritualism**.

- The early Church fought real sorcery, as seen in Acts 8:9–24 (Simon the Sorcerer) and Acts 19:19 (where new converts burned their magical books).

- Church Fathers like St. Augustine, St. John Chrysostom, and others spoke out against astrology, divination, and the occult.

- **Every official Catholic document to this day** (Catechism, Canon Law, exorcism rites) condemns witchcraft as mortal sin.

If Catholicism were truly "witchcraft," Satan would not wage a relentless 2,000-year war against it.

Satan's Counterfeits: Why Demons Fear the Church

Everything Satan offers is an inversion—a perversion—of something real and sacred:

- **Baptism** twisted into ritual curses and "un-baptism" ceremonies.

- **The Eucharist** is stolen, mocked, and desecrated in black masses.

- **Confession** counterfeited in "energy cleansings" and "shadow work."

- **Holy Orders** mocked through fake priestesses, mediums, and shamans.

Demons aren't afraid of your "positive vibes" or sage bundles. They don't tremble at crystals or wishful thinking. They tremble at **the authority of Christ** alive in **His Church**—especially when wielded through the Sacraments. Just ask a real Catholic exorcist. During a Rite of Exorcism, demons are forced to reveal this truth under obedience: they hate holy water, they recoil at the words of absolution, and they tremble when the Eucharist is present. **They recognize the authority of Christ passed down through His Church—and they know they have no power against it.**

Mark 16:17 says: "These signs will accompany those who believe: in my name they will drive out demons." And the Church Christ founded is the one that still drives out demons—*through His name and power.*

God's Warnings Against Witchcraft: Protection, Not Oppression

God's prohibitions against witchcraft, divination, and sorcery (Deuteronomy 18:10–12) are not acts of oppression or fear—**they are acts of protection**. God forbids these practices because they open the soul to real spiritual dangers that we, as finite human beings, cannot control or fully understand.

The spiritual world is not neutral, and not every spirit encountered is a friend. Demonic forces are fully capable of impersonating deceased loved ones, offering "hidden knowledge," or appearing harmless to lure a person deeper into bondage. St. Paul warns that **Satan himself "masquerades as an angel of light"** (2 Corinthians 11:14). Seeking secret knowledge through mediums, tarot cards, pendulums, "spirit guides," or so-called "ancestral contact" is not harmless curiosity—it is a breach of trust in God and **a door opened to spiritual deception**. Ask me how I know.

God's commandments against occult practices are thus like a loving parent warning a child not to play with fire or poisonous snakes. **It's not because He fears our empowerment**, but because He loves us too much to watch us burn ourselves with powers beyond our comprehension.

The Root of "Witchcraft"

The connection between sorcery and danger becomes even clearer when we look at the New Testament Greek word **_pharmakeia_** (φαρμακεία), often translated as "sorcery" or "witchcraft."

Pharmakeia is the root of our modern word "pharmacy," but in the biblical context it referred to **the use of potions, drugs, and occult rituals to alter consciousness or manipulate spiritual realities.** It was tied to deception, poisoning, spiritual rebellion, and the distortion of God's natural order. In Revelation 18:23, speaking of Babylon (symbol of the corrupt world system), Scripture says: "**...all nations were deceived by your sorcery (pharmakeia)."**

This is not mere superstition. God warns us that occult practices are spiritual poison—seeming to offer temporary "power" or "healing" but, in truth, **enslaving the soul** under demonic influence.

Real Witchcraft Recognizes Real Power

In the world of Craft, New Agers are often referred to as "fluffy bunnies" and they are typically trendy teenage emo girls who have no idea what it is to be a real witch. They are simply rebelling to rebel. But actual practitioners, particularly Satanists, know where true spiritual power lies.

At black masses (another ritual inversion mimicking the Catholic Church), the highest prize is the desecration of a **consecrated Eucharist.** They don't steal ordinary bread from the grocery store or the grape juice and crackers from the Protestant churches on every corner. **They risk everything to steal what Catholics believe to be the true Body of Christ.** They mock and profane what they fear because, even in their rebellion, they recognize the **Real Presence they hate.** If the Eucharist were merely a symbol, it wouldn't be worth stealing. Their hatred itself testifies to the truth: Christ is truly present in His Church—and the forces of darkness know it better than many of us do.

My Brief Journey from Darkness to Light

Ten years ago, I was a Luciferian occultist. I didn't believe in Satan—just physics, natural law, and self-will. **But God, in His mercy, rescued me.** He opened my eyes to the reality of spiritual warfare, to the lies I had believed, and to the truth that salvation is found only in Christ, through His Church.

For the decade I was involved in the occult, I never experienced anything obviously terrifying—and that was part of the **deception.**

Everything seemed harmless, even good. I thought I had found a higher logic, a deeper enlightenment, compared to the "simple-minded" Christianity I had left behind.

But when I finally walked away, **the truth revealed itself**. For six months, I faced relentless spiritual attacks, with several diabolical experiences that even my son and husband fearfully witnessed—a fear and a darkness I could not explain. Only through constant prayer and the Scriptures I had committed to memory from my Pentecostal experience did I survive.

The practices that once seemed innocent had opened real doors to evil. Logic had become my idol, and in thinking I was wiser than Christians, I had become the most foolish of all—**blind to the danger I had invited into my life**.

Witchcraft doesn't appear with chains at first. It offers curiosity, power, and hidden knowledge—until it demands **everything**. Only Christ has the power to break the chains once they're forged.

Conclusion: There Is No Counterfeit for the Cure

The Catholic Church is not pagan witchcraft—it is the cure for it.

Where witchcraft and the occult offer counterfeit power, counterfeit healing, and counterfeit "enlightenment," **the Church offers the real thing**: the true Sacraments, the true authority of Christ, and the true victory over the forces of darkness. Satan doesn't create anything; he only distorts what God has already made. **That's why so many practices in the occult are twisted parodies of Catholic realities**: baptism becomes "cleansing rituals," confession becomes "shadow work," the Eucharist is mocked in black masses. The Church isn't mimicking witchcraft. Witchcraft is mocking the Church.

God's commandments against sorcery, divination, and occultism are not about oppression—they are about **protection**. He forbids these practices because they open doors to spirits we cannot control, forces that disguise themselves as good but enslave the soul. As Scripture warns, *"Satan masquerades as an angel of light"* (2 Corinthians 11:14).

I lived this deception for nearly a decade. **Everything seemed harmless**—until I left it behind, and the attacks began. Only through constant prayer and the mercy of God was I set free. The chains of witchcraft are soft at first, but they harden over time. Without Christ, they cannot be broken.

The Catholic Church, founded by Christ Himself, stands as a fortress against these deceptions.

Her Sacraments are real. Her authority is divine. Her protection is enduring. She is not the enemy of truth—she is the Bride of Christ, and the gates of hell will not prevail against her.

If you are searching for light, healing, or spiritual truth, you will not find it in the occult. You will find it where it has always been: in the heart of Christ, alive in His Church.

Conspiracy Theories: Fact vs. Fiction

For two thousand years, the Catholic Church has stood—and for two thousand years, she has been slandered. Every generation invents new accusations or recycles old ones. In this chapter, we tackle some of the most persistent conspiracy theories, expose their flaws, and show why none of them threaten the truth of Christ's Bride, the Catholic Church.

The Catholic Church Is Pagan

Facts: As we discussed earlier, Catholic worship is not pagan but biblical in origin. God Himself commanded the use of incense (Exodus 30:7–9), vestments (Exodus 28), sacred altars (Exodus 27), and intercessory prayer (Tobit 12:12, Revelation 5:8). Catholicism fulfills, not replaces, God's Old Testament worship. **Witchcraft seeks power apart from God**; Catholic liturgy seeks union with God through the very means He established. The Church is the fulfillment of the Old Covenant, not a pagan counterfeit.

The Catholic Church Invented Pagan Holidays Like Christmas and Easter.

Facts: Christmas honors Christ's birth based on scriptural timing and ancient Christian tradition, **not** Saturnalia or any Roman pagan festival. Easter celebrates Christ's Resurrection, **not** pagan spring gods. Accusing the Church of "stealing pagan holidays" is not supported by history or Scripture—it's a **modern myth born of anti-Catholicism**, not fact.

Christmas:

The date of December 25th was not chosen because of pagan festivals but from theological and biblical reasoning:

- According to **Luke 1:26–36**, Mary conceived Jesus six months after Elizabeth conceived John the Baptist.

- Based on ancient Jewish tradition and early Christian calculations, John the Baptist's conception was associated with the Jewish feast of Yom Kippur (around September).

- If John was conceived in late September, he would be born around late June (**the Nativity of John the Baptist, celebrated June 24**).

- Jesus' conception (the Annunciation, March 25) would therefore point to His birth nine months later—around **December 25**.

Additionally, early Christians believed that **great men of God died on the same date as their conception**. Since Jesus' Passion was dated around March 25, His conception was logically tied to that date—and thus His Nativity nine months later.

The formal celebration of Christmas on December 25 was later connected to the dedication of important churches in Rome, especially the Basilica of St. Mary Major, reinforcing the solemnity of Christ's birth. In short, December 25th honors the mystery of the Incarnation based on biblical timelines, not sun god worship or winter solstice festivals.

Easter:

Easter has **nothing to do with paganism** either.

- Easter directly flows from the Jewish Passover (**Pesach**), which commemorates God's deliverance of Israel from Egypt.

- Jesus' Passion, death, and Resurrection occurred during Passover week (Matthew 26:17–28:10).

- Early Christians celebrated the Resurrection immediately after Passover, and this has continued unbroken to today.

The word "Easter" only appears in English and Germanic languages (deriving from *Eostre*, a springtime festival), but in Latin, Greek, and other languages, and most of the Christian world, the name for Easter is **Pascha**—directly derived from the Hebrew **Pesach** (Passover)—because Christ's death and Resurrection occurred during the Jewish Passover and fulfilled it (Luke 22:15–20; 1 Corinthians 5:7–8).

Easter is rooted in biblical history, specifically Christ's fulfillment of the Old Covenant—**not in pagan fertility rites**. Many Gnostics, Occultists, and even some Protestant denominations like the Seventh Day Adventists, and those in the Torah (Hebrew Roots) Movements, claim that Easter is a remake of the pagan goddess Ishtar. This is historically and linguistically **false**. "Easter" sounds similar to "Ishtar" in English, but they have no connection. The feast of the Resurrection was celebrated by Christians centuries before English even existed as a language. Easter is not a pagan fertility festival; it is the Christian celebration of Christ's victory over sin and death.

The Pope Is the Antichrist

Facts: The Antichrist, according to Scripture, denies Jesus Christ (1 John 2:22; 1 John 4:3). Every Pope boldly proclaims Jesus Christ as Lord and God. This theory originated during the Protestant Reformation and is historically rooted in political grievances, not biblical theology. The Pope, as the successor of Peter, fulfills Christ's command to "strengthen your brothers" (Luke 22:32). He is not Christ's enemy, but His servant.

The Vatican Controls the World Through Freemasonry and the Illuminati

Facts: Far from participating in secret world domination, **the Catholic Church has condemned Freemasonry since 1738** (*In Eminenti*

Apostolatus). Catholics are not allowed to become masons or join any other secret society. Freemasonry and similar secret societies are fundamentally at odds with Catholic teaching on truth, salvation, and the public witness of faith. Catholic social doctrine supports the dignity of the human person, religious liberty, and subsidiarity—not global domination. If the Church truly controlled the world, modern society would not be so fiercely anti-Catholic.

The Canadian "Mass Graves" of Indigenous Children

Facts: There have been **no mass graves** found at Canadian residential schools. Ground-penetrating radar indicated soil disturbances, but no bodies have been excavated. The sensational claims remain unproven even years later. Historical tragedies such as disease and poor sanitation at these schools should not be ignored—but claims of secret mass murders by the Church have no factual basis and serve political agendas rather than truth.

Bella Dodd and the Communists Infiltration into the Catholic Church

Facts: Bella Dodd warned that communists *intended* to infiltrate the Church, but she provided no verifiable names or evidence that they succeeded. Her congressional testimony focused largely on education, not on ecclesiastical offices. Human sin in the Church comes from human weakness, not necessarily from hidden communist agents. Christ promised that the Church would endure despite human failure (Matthew 16:18).

The Catholic Church Hid the Bible from the People

Facts: As addressed earlier, without the Catholic Church, there would be no Bible. The Scriptures were preserved by Catholic monks who painstakingly hand-copied manuscripts for centuries. Most people were illiterate until modern times, which is why the Church taught the faith through liturgy, preaching, sacred art, and music. **Far from hiding Scripture**, the Catholic Church made it accessible to every generation according to the means available.

The Catholic Church Is the Whore of Babylon Mentioned in Revelation

False: To say the Church is the "Whore of Babylon" described in Revelation 17, full of corruption and idolatry, is the sin of calumny and misunderstands both Scripture and history.

The "Whore of Babylon" in Revelation represents *Rome* **as a pagan, persecuting empire—not** the Catholic Church. At the time John wrote Revelation (~90 AD), the Catholic Church was a small, persecuted minority. It was **pagan Rome** that oppressed and martyred Christians— not Christians persecuting others!

In fact, early Christians—including Church Fathers like Tertullian— understood "Babylon" as a code name for the Roman Empire itself, which used violence, immorality, and idolatry to dominate the world.

Moreover:

- The true Church is described as **the Bride of Christ** (Revelation 21:2, Ephesians 5:25–27), holy and pure, not a harlot.

- Jesus promised that the gates of hell would not prevail against His Church (Matthew 16:18).

- Scripture warns about **false churches and sects** arising (2 Peter 2:1–3, 2 Timothy 4:3–4)—not the corruption of the one, true Church Christ Himself established.

Finally, the Catholic Church **canonized** the Book of Revelation in the first place—hardly something she would have done if it were secretly condemning herself! In short, the Whore of Babylon symbolizes *pagan Rome* and worldly corruption—**not** the Church Christ founded. Claiming the Catholic Church is the Whore of Babylon is an inversion of biblical prophecy and a slander against Christ's own Bride.

Side Note: Some Claim the Whore of Babylon is "the Zionists"

Some conspiracy theorists—especially those involved in anti-Semitic or anti-globalist movements—argue that the "Whore of Babylon" represents "Zionists" or "world Jewry," supposedly controlling global finance, media, and governments.

This is false and dangerous for several reasons:

1. **It Distorts Revelation's Original Context:**

   When St. John wrote Revelation (~90 AD), the Jewish people themselves were **persecuted minorities** under the Roman Empire. Revelation uses "Babylon" as a *code name* for pagan, imperial Rome, the dominant worldly power persecuting both Christians and Jews.

2. **It Promotes Anti-Semitism:**

   Blaming the Jewish people as a whole for "Babylon" echoes centuries-old prejudices that led to real-world atrocities (pogroms, ghettos, expulsions, and even the Holocaust). The Catholic Church **explicitly rejects** the idea that the Jewish people are collectively responsible for evil (see *Nostra Aetate*, Vatican II).

3. **Christian Zionism ≠ Biblical Israel:**

   Some conspiracy theories confuse modern secular political movements (like political Zionism) with biblical Israel. **They are not the same.** The Church teaches respect for the Jewish people as the original recipients of God's covenant (Romans 9–11), but it also upholds that salvation comes through Christ alone (John 14:6).

4. **The Whore Symbolizes Worldly, Apostate Power:**

The "Whore of Babylon" symbolizes **any worldly system**—political, cultural, religious—that seduces humanity away from God through luxury, violence, and idolatry.

In John's time, this was pagan Rome. In later ages, **it can apply to any anti-Christian system**, but it is not tied to any one race or ethnic group.

In summary, Revelation is primarily about spiritual realities, not ethnic scapegoating. The Catholic Church condemns **anti-Semitism as a grave sin**. The "Whore of Babylon" represents apostate, worldly corruption, not a single nationality or race.

The Catholic Church Hoards Wealth and Doesn't Help the Poor

Facts: The Catholic Church is the **largest charitable organization in the world**. Through Catholic charities, hospitals, schools, disaster relief agencies, and missionary work, the Church feeds, clothes, houses, educates, and heals millions—regardless of religion, race, or nationality.

- Catholic Relief Services alone operates in over 100 countries.

- Catholic hospitals make up around 15% of the healthcare system in the U.S. alone.

- Catholic parishes and religious orders quietly serve the poor every day, often without media attention.

As for the Vatican's so-called "wealth," it consists mostly of priceless cultural artifacts, which the Church preserves for all humanity, not liquid assets used for luxury. All priests take a vow of poverty. Here's a photo of where Pope Francis lived up until his death. Room 201 at the Vatican's Santa Marta residence:

The Vatican's Santa Marta residence in 2005. Eric VANDEVILLE - Getty Images

What About Pachamama

One accusation that sometimes comes up against the Catholic Church is that we've embraced idolatry—specifically, that during the 2019 Amazon Synod, the Vatican endorsed the worship of a pagan goddess named *Pachamama*. This has been used to claim that the Church is apostate, syncretistic, or spiritually compromised. Let's clear this up once and for all.

What Actually Happened?

At the **Amazon Synod** in October 2019, a **ceremonial planting of a tree** took place in the Vatican gardens to highlight care for creation and the plight of Indigenous people. Present at this event were **carved wooden figures**—depicting **a pregnant woman**, often interpreted as a symbol of **life, fertility, motherhood, or creation** in Indigenous art.

Some online voices immediately labeled the image *Pachamama*—an Incan earth goddess—and claimed idolatry had occurred.

However, the Vatican clarified that the figure **was not worshiped**, nor was it intended to represent a pagan deity. It was a **cultural symbol** of life and fertility, not a divine object of Catholic devotion.

Some of the Indigenous participants at the Synod actually saw the statue as a representation of the **Blessed Virgin Mary**, inculturated within their own artistic tradition as *Our Lady of the Amazon*, protector of life and creation. The figure was not labeled a goddess by the Vatican, nor was it presented for worship. It was later critics who imposed the title *Pachamama* and accused the Church of idolatry.

What the Indigenous Community Actually Said:

The **Indigenous Catholics** who brought the image to the Vatican during the 2019 Amazon Synod **did not intend it as a pagan goddess**. Many of them **saw the figure as a representation of life and motherhood**, and **some explicitly identified her as a cultural depiction of the Blessed Virgin Mary**—especially **Mary as the Mother of All Living** and **protector of creation**.

This isn't new. Around the world, **local expressions of Mary often reflect the cultural imagery** of the people—Our Lady of Guadalupe in Mexico, Our Lady of La Vang in Vietnam, Our Lady of Kibeho in Rwanda. These aren't pagan goddesses; they are inculturated images of *the same Mary*, who brings Christ to every people. Americans seem to sometimes forget that the world doesn't revolve around us.

In the case of the Amazon Synod, some of the Indigenous participants understood the statue as an artistic symbol of **Our Lady of the Amazon**, much like the Madonna of Guadalupe wears Indigenous features and clothing. The figure was not formally canonized, approved for liturgical use, or named "Pachamama" by the Vatican—it was a **contextual symbol of fertility, life, and maternal care**, possibly viewed through a Marian lens by those who brought it.

Pope Francis later apologized not for idolatry—but for the **disrespect** shown when individuals **stole the statues and threw them into the Tiber River**. He confirmed there was **no idolatrous intent**, and the figures were used as part of a **contextual, symbolic expression** of life and creation—not as objects of worship.

The **Catechism of the Catholic Church** is crystal clear:

"Idolatry not only refers to false pagan worship. It remains a constant temptation. Idolatry consists in divinizing what is not God."—CCC 2113

The Church condemns idolatry unequivocally. Catholics worship **God alone**—Father, Son, and Holy Spirit. We **venerate** saints and honor cultural expressions of faith, but **we never worship images, statues, or symbols.** (Remember, worship requires sacrifice. Honor and praise is not worship.)

This was **not an endorsement of paganism**. It was an attempt—perhaps clumsy, but not heretical—to incorporate cultural imagery into a call for ecological and spiritual renewal. The image was **not canonized**, approved for worship, or placed in any liturgical role. And no doctrine changed.

Criticism of the event may be fair. Conspiratorial claims that "Rome has fallen" are not.

As Catholics, we must hold fast to the truth with **discernment and charity**. That includes resisting reactionary fear-mongering and remembering that the **Church, while filled with flawed people, is still protected by the Holy Spirit** and will never teach error in faith or morals (cf. Matthew 16:18, John 16:13).

Conclusion: Through the Lens of Truth and Trust

The Catholic Church has never claimed to be a collection of perfect people—only that she was founded by a perfect Savior. Yes, scandals have happened. Yes, there have been corrupt clergy, cover-ups, and painful betrayals. These wounds must be acknowledged, mourned, and healed. But the failures of individuals do **not undo the promises of Christ**.

Jesus didn't say, "Follow my Church as long as its leaders are flawless." He said, *"I will build my Church, and the gates of hell shall not prevail against it"* (Matthew 16:18). He chose to build His Kingdom through broken men, and He promised that the **Holy Spirit would preserve the Church in truth**, even when some within her fall.

Conspiracy theories—like the Pachamama accusations—prey on fear, mistrust, and misinformation. They often lack context, twist reality, and replace authentic concern with **spiritual paranoia**. They distract from the real mission: proclaiming Christ, receiving the Sacraments, and living the Gospel.

Our response to scandal must be twofold: **righteous accountability and unshakable fidelity**. We do not excuse sin, but neither do we abandon the Bride of Christ because some members have failed. When you find rot in the branches, you prune—you don't cut down the whole tree.

We must remember that the Church is not just a human institution—it is a divine one. It is the **ark of salvation**, not because her crew is sinless, but because her Captain is. The faith is not built on the holiness of popes, bishops, or priests—it is built on the rock, who is Christ.

Just as we wouldn't publicly trash our spouse's character in front of others—especially those who don't know them well—we should exercise the same care when speaking about the Church, particularly the Holy Father. Criticism within the family of faith is sometimes necessary, but airing accusations carelessly or disrespectfully can lead to **scandal**, which Scripture warns against (cf. Matthew 18:6). We are called to build up the Body of Christ, not tear it down for rhetorical points or social

CONSPIRACY THEORIES: FACT VS. FICTION

media outrage. If we truly believe the Church is the Bride of Christ, then we should speak of her—and her shepherds—with the reverence due to something sacred, even when correction is warranted. Truth and charity must go hand in hand.

So don't flee the Church. **Fight for her. Heal within her. Worship Christ in her.** And when scandal or confusion shakes your trust, don't look to the headlines or the hashtags. Look to the tabernacle. **That's where the truth still lives.**

This Scripture really spoke to me regarding conspiracy theories and events beyond my control:

> "My child, perform your tasks with **humility**;
> then you will be loved by those whom God accepts.
> The greater you are, the more you must **humble yourself**;
> so you will find favor in the sight of the Lord.
> For great is the might of the Lord,
> but by the **humble he is glorified.**
> **Do not seek what is too difficult for you**
> **or investigate what is beyond your power.**
> **Reflect on what you have been commanded,**
> **for what is hidden is not your concern.**
> **Do not meddle in matters that are beyond you,**
> **for more than you can understand has been shown to you.**
> For their **conceit** has led many astray,
> and **wrong opinion has impaired their judgment.**
> Without eyes there is no **light**;
> without knowledge there is no **wisdom.**
> **A stubborn mind will come to a bad end,**
> and whoever loves danger will perish in it."
> —*Sirach 3:17–29, NRSVue*

Conclusion: The Indestructible Church

The Catholic Church has been falsely accused for two millennia, and still she stands. Empires rise and fall. Nations collapse. Cultures rot from within. But the Church endures because she is not a merely human institution; **she is divine in origin**. Every generation invents new lies. Every generation sees them collapse. Christ Himself promised: *"The gates of hell shall not prevail against it"* (Matthew 16:18).

The Church does not need to fear lies. Truth always outlasts slander. And the Catholic Church, wounded though her members may be, **will endure until the end of time**, because she is the Body of Christ on earth. But we, her children, have a grave responsibility. In an age when rumors spread faster than truth, we are called not only to resist repeating falsehoods but to **actively defend** the Church of Jesus Christ with truth, charity, and courage.

Scripture warns us: *"I tell you, on the day of judgment people will render an account for every careless word they speak"* (Matthew 12:36).

It is no small thing to slander the Bride of Christ, even by careless repetition. It is no small thing to remain silent while others do. **Before believing or repeating accusations against the Church, we owe it to Christ Himself to seek the truth**—diligently, humbly, and prayerfully. We must do our due diligence in honest research and *"Study to show yourself approved unto God, a workman who need not to be ashamed, rightly dividing the word of truth"* (2 Timothy 2:15).

The Crusades and the Spanish Inquisition: Setting the Record Straight

Few episodes in Church history are as misunderstood—or as weaponized—as the Crusades and the Spanish Inquisition. Today, they are often presented as proof that the Catholic Church is violent, oppressive, and corrupt. **But when we step outside of modern stereotypes and actually examine the facts, a very different picture emerges**.

Were there mistakes made by individuals? Absolutely—as there always are when fallen human beings are involved. But at their core, the Crusades and the Inquisition were *defensive efforts*, **not offensive campaigns of conquest**. They were responses to real threats, and without them, Western civilization—and Christianity itself—may not have survived.

Understanding the Crusades

In the centuries leading up to the Crusades, Islamic forces had conquered vast swaths of historically Christian territory across the Middle East, North Africa, and Spain. **Christians, who had thrived across these lands since apostolic times, faced persecution, forced conversions, slavery, and death. Holy sites were desecrated**. Pilgrimages became dangerous, and often fatal.

By the late eleventh century, the Byzantine Empire, the last major Christian stronghold in the East, was under siege. Pope Urban II's call for the First Crusade in 1095 was not a call for conquest—**it was a plea for defense. Christians were asked to lay down their lives to**

protect their brethren, to reclaim sacred ground, and to prevent the total collapse of Christian civilization.

The Crusades were a defensive war, fought reluctantly, not a land grab. Without them, Europe itself might have fallen under Islamic domination, and the Americas may never have been evangelized at all.

Were there atrocities? Sadly, yes. **War always brings suffering.** But these tragedies do not erase the just cause at the heart of the Crusades: the defense of faith, family, and freedom, and protection of the innocent. **Under Islamic regimes, Christians became second-class citizens—** *dhimmis*—forced to pay heavy taxes (*jizya*) simply for the right to live. They were forbidden to publicly practice their faith, build new churches, or even repair existing ones. Public expressions of Christianity, like carrying a cross or ringing church bells, were banned. In many places, Christians could not testify in court against a Muslim, meaning they had **no legal protection against violence or injustice.**

Forced conversions were common, and refusal often meant imprisonment, enslavement, or execution. **Christian women were especially vulnerable**, subject to abduction and forced marriage. Entire villages were massacred for resisting Islamic rule. This was not merely "political tension"—it was systemic, religiously-driven oppression designed to **eradicate Christianity from the lands where it was born.** The Crusaders were not invading peaceful kingdoms; they were responding to centuries of conquest, persecution, and the real threat of Christian annihilation.

Understanding the Spanish Inquisition

The Spanish Inquisition, too, is often painted as a mindless reign of terror. But the truth is far more complex.

Following the Reconquista—Spain's 700-year struggle to reclaim Christian lands from Muslim rule—the country faced deep social and religious instability. Many recent converts (both Jewish and Muslim) continued to practice their former faiths secretly, undermining the fragile new unity of Christian Spain. The Inquisition was not about punishing sincere believers. It was a legal tribunal tasked with investigating cases of heresy and preventing civil unrest in a society still deeply scarred by centuries of religious conflict.

Contrary to popular myth:

- Torture was rare, regulated, and far less brutal than in secular courts.

- Executions were extremely rare compared to other European legal systems.

- The Inquisition often acted more leniently than royal or feudal courts of the time.

The Spanish Inquisition was imperfect—as every human institution is—but it was not the indiscriminate bloodbath it's often portrayed as. **None of this is to excuse the real instances of injustice, torture, or bloodshed that did occur during the Spanish Inquisition. Sinful actions must always be acknowledged for what they are.** However, we must also resist the temptation to judge the past by the standards of today. Medieval Europe was a far different world, a time when survival, stability, and religious unity were seen as essential to social order. Projecting modern ideas of individual rights and secular governance onto a time and place that had no concept of either is not historical honesty; it is arrogance.

Myth vs. Fact: Crusades and Inquisition

Myth	Fact
The Crusades were greedy land-grabs by bloodthirsty Christians.	The Crusades were defensive wars to protect Christian lands, lives, and faith against centuries of Muslim aggression.
Christians invaded peaceful Muslim lands unprovoked.	By 1095, Muslim forces had already conquered two-thirds of the Christian world. The Crusades were a response to ongoing attacks and persecutions.
The Spanish Inquisition killed millions of innocent people.	Modern historians estimate around 3,000–5,000 executions over 350 years—far fewer than secular courts at the same time.
Torture was rampant and brutal during the Inquisition.	Torture was strictly regulated, used infrequently, and less severe than in most secular courts of the era.
The Church used the Inquisition for power and wealth.	The Inquisition's primary goal was religious unity and civil peace in a fragile post-Reconquista society. It operated under strict guidelines, not arbitrary greed.

Conclusion: Defense, Not Domination

The Catholic Church is made up of sinners, yet she is also protected by divine promise: *"The gates of hell shall not prevail against it"* (Matthew 16:18). The Crusades and the Spanish Inquisition **were not perfect—** no human endeavor ever is. But they were not the senseless atrocities modern myths claim. They were imperfect but **necessary efforts to defend the Church,** her people, and the future of Christian civilization itself.

Had Christians in those centuries refused to act, the Church—and everything built upon her foundation—might have been swept away. America itself, founded centuries later, would likely be a very different place, and not one founded on Christian principles. The survival of the Church through these trials is not a mark of shame. It is proof that God protects His Church, even through the weakness of her members.

East vs. West:
Why I Didn't Stop at Eastern Orthodoxy

My Time in Eastern Orthodoxy

I spent over a year immersing myself in the writings of the Church Fathers and was deeply drawn to the ancient faith preserved in Eastern Orthodoxy. Apostolic succession made sense—it was clear that the early Church didn't just believe in authority; they lived under it. I had been attending an Eastern Orthodox church and was ready to commit as a catechumen toward chrismation… but I kept feeling a gentle, yet persistent nudge from God.

I told myself I had done my due diligence in study of the papacy, the *Filioque*, and the role of Mary as *Theotokos*—God-bearer. But the Lord wouldn't allow me to move forward until I really got honest with myself and admitted that it deserved a deep dive, just as I had given to the East.

At the same time, I was recently remarried after being a single mother for much of my life and struggling to fully embrace my husband's God-given role as the head of our home. That inner resistance led me to a surprising realization: **God always works through hierarchy**. In the home, in the Church, in civil governments—even in nature, there is a divinely ordered structure. And as much as I had healed, I saw that part of my heart was still resisting rightful authority. That quiet rebellion—however subtle—was a red flag. As Scripture says, *"The heart is deceitful above all things… who can understand it?"* (Jer. 17:9).

That's when it hit me: **marriage doesn't have two heads**—or ten. It has one. Christ is the Bridegroom of the Church, and He didn't leave her with a group marriage arrangement. The bishops are not all equal spouses. Just as my home needs a head, so does Christ's Church. And He made that head visible in Peter. The Orthodox Church preserves apostolic succession and the beauty of the ancient faith—but without the head, unity breaks down. And unity isn't optional—it's the desire of Christ's heart (John 17:21).

So I reopened my study. I prayed. A lot. My flesh wanted to go East because I loved the aesthetics, the prayers, the beautiful and reverent Divine Liturgy of John Chrysostom. And it would've been much easier for me to remain comfortably where I was and pursue confirmation, because the Eastern Orthodox allow up to three marriages, meaning I wouldn't have to wait for annulments before receiving Sacraments. But I promised God I would follow His lead no matter where it took me. I asked hard questions. And He brought me, at last, not just to the ancient faith, but to **its fullness** in the Catholic Church. I love and pray for reunification with our brothers and sisters from the East. Until then, let's look at where we differ and what we have in common.

What We Share

- Valid Sacraments (Eucharist and Holy Orders)
- Apostolic succession
- Deep reverence for liturgy and tradition
- Veneration of Mary and the saints
- Honor for Church Fathers and Councils
- The Real Presence of Christ in the Eucharist

"The Orthodox Church is a true Church—but a wounded one, because it is separated from the visible unity Christ desires."—CCC 838 (paraphrased)

So what's missing?

The Keys to the Kingdom: The Papacy

- Jesus gave **Peter** the keys (Matt 16:18-19), not just to "a" Church but to **the** Church.

- Early Church Fathers (even Eastern ones like St. John Chrysostom) affirmed the primacy of Rome.

- Ecumenical councils were historically validated only **with Rome's approval**.

- Without the Pope, the Orthodox have **no visible, unifying authority**, leading to national churches with doctrinal differences (e.g., contraception, remarriage, calendar).

St. Maximus the Confessor (seventh century, Orthodox saint) stated:

"All the churches everywhere **must agree with the Roman Church**, for it has always been the guardian of apostolic tradition."

The Magisterium

- The Orthodox reject a centralized teaching office. So when disputes arise (e.g., divorce, moral teachings), they don't have a **final arbiter**.

- Catholicism has the **Magisterium** to protect unity of truth.

Doctrinal Development

- The Orthodox often accuse Catholics of adding doctrine (e.g., Immaculate Conception, purgatory).

- But truth develops as it's more deeply understood—not invented.

- Example: The Trinity wasn't formally articulated until centuries after Christ, but the seed was there.

The Tragedy of Schism

- The East broke from Peter in 1054.

- Jesus prayed in John 17 that we "may all be one."

- Division is a wound in Christ's Body, and schism is a grave sin (see CCC 2089).

- Love for the East includes the desire for *reunion*, not division.

The Authority of the Church

- Christ established **one** Church (Eph. 4:4–5), not a loose federation of apostolic churches.

- That one Church is visible, hierarchical, and sacramental.

- The Catholic Church, under the successor of Peter, is the **fullness** of that Church.

The **Filioque** clause—Latin for "and the Son"—has been one of the most famous theological points of dispute between the Catholic and Eastern Orthodox Churches. But once you dig into the **Scriptures**, **Church Fathers**, and the **theology of the Trinity**, it becomes clear that the Catholic Church didn't corrupt the Creed—it clarified a truth that was already there.

What Is the *Filioque?*

The original **Nicene Creed** (325 AD), expanded in **381 AD** at the First Council of Constantinople, states:

> "We believe in the Holy Spirit, the Lord, the giver of life, who proceeds from the Father."

- Later, in the **sixth century**, Western Christians—starting in Spain—added the phrase **"and the Son"** (*Filioque*) to clarify that the Holy Spirit proceeds **from the Father *and* the Son.**

- It was officially included in the Latin Church's recitation of the Creed by the eleventh century.

- The **Eastern Orthodox** objected to both the **theology** and the **unauthorized modification** of the Creed.

Why Did Catholics Add It?

Because heresies were creeping in—particularly Arianism and subordinationism—and the Western Church saw the need to reinforce the **full divinity** of the Son by showing that the Spirit proceeds from **both** the Father and the Son **as from one principle.**

Biblical Evidence for *Filioque*

The Bible doesn't use the word *Filioque*, but the concept is clearly present:

- John 15:26 (Jesus speaking):

   "When the Advocate comes, whom **I will send to you from the Father**, the Spirit of truth **who proceeds from the Father**, he will testify about me."

   Here, the Spirit **proceeds from the Father** but is **sent by the Son**, implying shared origin or mutual relationship.

- Galatians 4:6:

   "God has sent the Spirit of his Son into our hearts, crying, 'Abba! Father!'"

   The Spirit is called the **Spirit of the Son.**

- Romans 8:9:

"Anyone who does not have the **Spirit of Christ** does not belong to him."

The Holy Spirit is referred to as the *Spirit of the Father* **and** the *Spirit of the Son*—showing a dual relationship.

What Did the Church Fathers Say?

Even many **Eastern Fathers** expressed a *Filioque*-style theology **long before** the controversy:

- **St. Cyril of Alexandria** (fifth century):

"The Spirit proceeds from the Father and receives from the Son."

- **St. Epiphanius of Salamis** (fourth century):

"The Holy Spirit is from the Father and the Son; not made, not created, but proceeding."

- **St. Hilary of Poitiers** (fourth century, West):

"The Spirit is from the Father and the Son."

- **St. Augustine** (clearest Western expression):

"The Holy Spirit proceeds from the Father *and the Son* as from one principle."

Theological Reasoning: One Principle, Not Two

The Catholic Church teaches that the Spirit proceeds **from the Father and the Son together as from a single source** (see Catechism 246–248). This protects the unity of the Trinity:

- **One nature** → One divine will → One divine action

- Therefore, the Spirit's eternal procession reflects **oneness** of Father and Son, not duality.

The Orthodox fear that *Filioque* makes the Son a second cause or origin, but Catholics clarify: **the Spirit does not proceed from the Son independently** but **from the Father through the Son**, or **from both as one principle.**

To summarize:

- The **Filioque** affirms the **shared divinity** and **oneness** of Father and Son.

- It has **biblical and patristic support**, especially in the West.

- The Church added it **not to change doctrine**, but to **defend truth** in the face of heresy.

- The issue is more about **authority and clarity** than a contradiction of faith.

Moral Shifts

It's also worth noting that while many admire the Eastern Orthodox Church for preserving ancient liturgy and spiritual beauty, **aesthetics alone do not define the true Church.** Just because something *looks* ancient doesn't mean it holds to the fullness of the truth. In recent decades, many Orthodox jurisdictions have taken **alarming moral turns**—openly permitting **contraception**, and in some cases, tolerating or even permitting **in vitro fertilization (IVF)**. For example, the **Orthodox Church in America (OCA)** states that "under certain circumstances" the use of contraception may be permitted with pastoral guidance (OCA website – Orthodox Church and Birth Control). Similarly, some Orthodox bioethics statements argue that IVF may be morally acceptable when the embryo is not discarded or destroyed, such as the position outlined in *Bioethics and the Orthodox Church* by H. Tristram Engelhardt Jr.

These aren't peripheral issues. They go to the heart of human dignity, marriage, and the sanctity of life. In contrast, the **Catholic Church stands alone in maintaining a consistent, authoritative moral witness**, rooted in both Scripture and natural law. *Humanae Vitae* (1968), Pope Paul VI's landmark encyclical, reaffirmed that *"each and every marital act must of necessity retain its intrinsic relationship to the procreation of human life"* (HV 11). The Church also unequivocally teaches that IVF, even with good intentions, violates the dignity of the person and the conjugal act (*Catechism of the Catholic Church*, 2376–2377).

The sign of the true Church isn't simply a beautiful liturgy—it's the ability to **preserve truth without compromise**, even when it's hard to hear.

Conclusion: Why the One True Church Is Roman Catholic

I loved my time in the Eastern Orthodox Church. It taught me to be present, to breathe in the mystery, to stand in awe before the altar. But as beautiful as the icons were, as powerful as the chants echoed, I kept bumping into the same question: *Who is the final authority on matters of faith and doctrine when Bishops disagree?* The more I studied, the more I prayed, the clearer it became: the early Church didn't just honor Rome—they *depended* on it. **Without the Pope, there was no final say, no safeguard against division, no center to the circle.**

Orthodoxy has much of the treasure—but not the keys. And Jesus gave those keys to **Peter**.

In the end, while Eastern Orthodoxy holds much beauty, reverence, and apostolic truth, it stops just short of fullness. It preserves the form but not the fullness of the Church Christ established. Without union with the successor of Peter, the Orthodox churches remain in a state of schism—still valid in many ways but lacking the visible head Christ intended to unite His Bride. The dispute over the *Filioque*, like the rejection of papal primacy, ultimately **reflects a deeper resistance to authority**—something I had to confront not only theologically but personally. God does not build disorder; He builds a Kingdom with structure, headship, and unity. Just as a family is not led by multiple husbands, Christ's Church is not meant to function with competing bishops. There is one Bridegroom and one visible head of His Bride on earth. The more I studied, prayed, and submitted my heart, the clearer it became: the Catholic Church is not just *a* church—it is **the Church**. The One, Holy, Catholic, and Apostolic Church that Christ founded. At last, I came home to Rome.

If you'd like a deeper dive into the East vs. West debate, I'd recommend *Answering Orthodoxy: A Catholic Response to Attacks from the East* by Michael Lofton, and Erick Ybarra's *The Papacy: Revisiting the Debate Between Catholics and Orthodox.*

Putting It All Together: A Walk Through the Mass

The Mass: Heaven's Liturgy on Earth

Many non-Catholics see the Mass as a lifeless ritual. Stand up, sit down, mumble some prayers. But once you begin to understand the meaning behind each movement, each word, each posture, you realize you're stepping into something far greater than you could ever imagine.

The Catholic Mass isn't man-made tradition—it's divine liturgy, rooted in Scripture and prefigured in the Jewish temple. It is both **the fulfillment of Old Testament worship** and **a participation in the eternal worship of heaven,** as described in the Book of Revelation.

Let's walk through the Mass, not as spectators, but with eyes open to what is truly taking place.

The Mass Follows a Heavenly and Temple-Based Structure

The Mass is divided into **two main parts:**

1. **Liturgy of the Word**–rooted in the **synagogue service,** where Scripture was read and interpreted.

2. **Liturgy of the Eucharist**–rooted in the **temple worship,** where sacrifice was offered by a priest.

Just as Jewish worship moved from hearing the Word to offering the Lamb, so does the Catholic Mass—from proclaiming the Gospel to offering the **Lamb of God** on the altar. (Remember, Christ came to fulfill, not to eliminate.)

Introductory Rites: Entering Sacred Space

The Mass begins with a **procession**—mirroring the entrance of the high priest into the Holy Place. The priest approaches the altar, **bows** or **genuflects**, and kisses it. Why? Because the altar represents Christ and will soon hold the sacrifice of Calvary.

We begin with the **Sign of the Cross**, marking ourselves with the Trinitarian name—a declaration of identity and purpose.

Then comes the **Penitential Act**, where we prepare our hearts:

"I confess to almighty God…"

During the **Confiteor**, we say:

"Through my fault, through my fault, through my most grievous fault," while striking our chest (**mea culpa**) in a physical expression of repentance. This gesture is rooted in **Luke 18:13**, where the tax collector beat his breast, saying, *"God, be merciful to me, a sinner."*

This is not empty ritual—it's purification before sacrifice, just as the Old Testament priests washed and cleansed before entering God's presence.

Liturgy of the Word: God Speaks

We then hear readings from:

- The **Old Testament**–foreshadowing Christ.

- A **Psalm**–often chanted, in keeping with ancient Jewish tradition.

- A **New Testament epistle**–teaching the early Church.

- The **Gospel**–the high point, where we stand in reverence and sing *"Alleluia."*

We sign our foreheads, lips, and hearts with a cross: *"May the Word of the Lord be on my mind, on my lips, and in my heart."* The deacon or priest kisses the Gospel book, just as the ancient Jews revered the Torah scrolls.

The **homily** breaks open the Word, like Ezra and the Levites in Nehemiah 8, giving understanding to the people.

Then we recite the **Creed**, our public profession of faith once delivered to the saints (Jude 1:3). When we say *"By the power of the Holy Spirit, He was incarnate of the Virgin Mary and became man,"* we bow in reverence—acknowledging the miracle of the Incarnation.

Liturgy of the Eucharist: The New Passover

Now begins the part of the Mass that mirrors the **Jewish temple sacrifice**—but with one critical difference. Instead of offering animals, the priest offers the **Lamb of God** Himself.

We present gifts of bread and wine during the **Offertory**—but what we're really placing on the altar is ourselves: our prayers, sacrifices, and intentions.

The priest then says:

> *"Pray, brethren, that my sacrifice and yours may be acceptable to God, the almighty Father."*

This reminds us: **it's not just the priest's sacrifice—it's ours too.**

The Eucharistic Prayer begins with the **Sanctus**:

> *"Holy, holy, holy Lord..."*

This echoes **Isaiah 6** and **Revelation 4**—the worship of angels in heaven. We are joining that same heavenly liturgy.

Consecration: The Miracle at the Heart of the Mass

At the heart of the Mass is the **consecration**. The priest, in the person of Christ, speaks the very words Jesus said at the Last Supper:

"This is My Body... This is the chalice of my blood..."

This is the moment of **transubstantiation**—a word that describes the change in substance. While the appearance (or "accidents") of bread and wine remain, the essence becomes Christ Himself. This is not symbolic. It is a **literal, mystical, and sacramental reality**.

The priest then **elevates** the consecrated host and chalice. Many Catholics bow their heads or whisper quietly, *"My Lord and my God,"* echoing St. Thomas in John 20:28.

Bells are often rung, just as they were in the temple (Exodus 28:33–35) to mark sacred moments.

The Great Amen: Our Seal of Faith

After the doxology—*"Through Him, with Him, and in Him..."*—the people respond with a resounding **"Amen."** This is not a casual ending. It's our **bold assent** to everything that just occurred. In Jewish tradition, the "Great Amen" **sealed the covenant**. Here, it affirms our belief in **Christ truly present**.

Communion: Receiving the Lamb

We pray the **Our Father**, the perfect prayer taught by Jesus Himself, and offer one another a **Sign of Peace**, acknowledging we must be reconciled before approaching the altar (cf. Matthew 5:23–24).

Then comes the **Fraction Rite**—the priest breaks the host, just as Christ's body was broken. We sing:

"Lamb of God, you take away the sins of the world..."

This recalls **John 1:29** and the **Passover Lamb**, whose bones were not broken but who was sacrificed for the salvation of the people.

We approach for **Holy Communion** by bowing or genuflecting in reverence. We are not taking a symbol. We are receiving **Jesus Himself**. Those who are in attendance but not Catholic may approach with arms crossed in an X (palms to shoulder) and receive a blessing from the priest.

Closing Rites: Sent on Mission

After a moment of thanksgiving, the priest blesses the people and sends us forth:

> *"Go forth, the Mass is ended."*

The Latin **"Ite, missa est"** means *"You are sent."* We are being commissioned—transformed by Christ, now carrying Him into the world.

The Mass Is the Fulfillment of Jewish Worship

The structure of the Mass fulfills and transcends the Old Covenant:

- **Synagogue → Liturgy of the Word**
- **Temple Sacrifice → Liturgy of the Eucharist**
- **Passover Meal → Eucharistic Feast**

Jesus didn't abolish ritual—He **fulfilled it**. The Mass is not the rejection of religion; it is religion in its purest, divinely instituted form.

Conclusion: The Lamb at the Center

At the center of it all is Jesus Christ, truly present in the Eucharist. Not a symbol. Not a reminder. Not a motivational speech with emotional music. The same Jesus who was born in Bethlehem (which means "house of bread"), who multiplied loaves, who said, *"Unless you eat* *my flesh and drink my blood...*" (John 6), now comes to us under the form of bread and wine.

Every bow, every word, every chant in the Mass is designed to draw our attention to **Him**.

If you want to know where heaven touches earth, look no further than the Catholic Mass. It is the wedding feast of the Lamb—**and you are invited**.

Final Thoughts

As we come to the end of this journey, I hope you see that becoming Catholic isn't about abandoning a relationship with Jesus for a legalistic religion. It's about stepping into the **fullness** of that relationship—embracing everything He gave us for our salvation, our sanctification, and our spiritual nourishment.

This book didn't begin as an academic project. It began as a deeply personal search for truth. And if there's one thread running through every page, it's this:

I became Catholic because it's true.

The Catholic Church is not just one denomination among many. It is **pre-denominational**—the Church Christ Himself founded—built upon the apostles, with Peter as its visible head. From the beginning, it has borne the four essential marks: **One, Holy, Catholic, and Apostolic.** These aren't slogans or lofty ideals. They are the identity—and the proof—of the true Church.

We explored the authority Jesus gave to Peter—the keys of the Kingdom—rooted in the Old Testament structure of the Davidic monarchy. We saw how **apostolic succession** continues that authority today, through bishops ordained in an **unbroken line** stretching back to the apostles. The Magisterium isn't man-made. It's Christ's voice, safeguarded by the Holy Spirit. Without it, Christianity fragments into personal opinions and doctrinal chaos. Just look around at modern Christianity.

We uncovered the Jewish roots of our faith and saw how Catholicism fulfills—not rejects—the Old Covenant. Jesus is the **New Adam**, Mary the **New Eve**, the Eucharist the **New Passover**. The papacy and Marian teachings aren't medieval additions. They are **biblical, historical, and deeply rooted in the life of the early Church.**

We examined that early Church—not as a formless community of well-meaning believers, but as a liturgical, hierarchical, sacramental body united under bishops in communion with Rome. Their worship was centered on the Eucharist. Their faith was apostolic. They baptized for the forgiveness of sins, confessed those sins aloud, venerated martyrs, **and submitted to the Church** as both mother and teacher. They were Catholic.

We addressed the canon of Scripture and dismantled the myth that the Bible existed before the Church. It was the **Catholic Church that preserved, discerned, and canonized** the Scriptures. Without her, there would be no Bible as we know it. And the Protestant Reformers didn't just retranslate—they edited words, **removed books,** and undermined the very authority that gave us the Bible in the first place.

We stood before the mystery of the **Eucharist**—the source and summit of Christian life. Jesus didn't speak metaphorically in John 6. He said, *"My flesh is real food, and my blood is real drink."* The early Church believed Him. **The Fathers defended it. The martyrs died for it.** And at every Mass, Catholics receive Christ—Body, Blood, Soul, and Divinity. Not a symbol. A sacrament.

We clarified the misunderstood practice of praying to saints and honoring Mary—not as rivals to Christ, but as members of His Body who intercede for us, just like our friends on earth do. We don't worship them—we **venerate** them, because they are already perfected in heaven and united with us in Christ.

We tackled the modern breakdown of authority in Protestantism—how the rejection of apostolic hierarchy has led not to reform but to **fragmentation**: hundreds to thousands of denominations, contradictory doctrines, and worship shaped more by personal taste than timeless truth. Meanwhile, the Catholic Church has remained doctrinally united for 2,000 years, not because of human perfection, but because of **divine protection.**

We reexamined **worship**—not as performance, but as sacrifice. In the Old Covenant, worship always involved a priest, an altar, and a sacrifice. And in the New Covenant, we still have all three. The Mass isn't a sermon or a concert. It's the **re-presentation of Calvary**—the once-for-all sacrifice of Christ, made present again across time and space.

Even Eastern Orthodoxy, with all its beauty and apostolic roots, fell short for me. Without a visible, unifying head—the successor of Peter—Orthodoxy remains fragmented across national and ethnic lines, unable to speak with one voice in matters of faith and morals. The same resistance to authority that once lived in my own heart, I saw mirrored there. Christ didn't design His Church to be leaderless or divided. He gave the keys to Peter—for unity, not control.

So—why become Catholic?

Not because it's emotional.
Not because it's cultural.
Not because it's comfortable.
Because it's true.

If something stirred in you while reading this book—if you felt even a flicker of the possibility that there's more to the Church than you were taught—don't ignore it. **Ask God to show you the fullness of truth**—without fear, without filter, and without agenda.

That's what I did. I laid down my pride, my pain, and my preconceptions. I asked God to lead me to the Church He founded.

And He did.

He didn't hand me a prosperity gospel franchise or a church of convenience. He gave me a home—rooted in history, sustained by grace, and overflowing with sacramental gifts. My prayer is that this book has opened your eyes to what I finally saw: The Catholic Church is not just one Christian option among many. It is the Church Jesus established. It is the Church built on Peter, guided by the Holy Spirit, and still proclaiming the same Gospel after 2,000 years—not perfectly by human hands, but infallibly by divine promise.

Come home.
You are loved.
You are wanted.
Because it's true.
And the fullness of faith and truth awaits you.

One Last Thing...

Dear Seeker of Truth,

Thank you so much for taking the time to read *Because It's True*. Whether you are just beginning to explore the Catholic faith or are well along the journey, I hope this book deepened your understanding, stirred your heart, and brought you closer to the One who is Truth Himself.

This work was a labor of love, born from years of searching, study, struggle, and ultimately, profound peace in coming home to the Catholic Church. My prayer is that it serves as a faithful witness to the beauty, depth, and authority of the Church Jesus Christ founded.

If this book blessed or encouraged you in any way, I would be deeply grateful if you would consider leaving a review. Your honest feedback not only helps others discover the book but also supports this mission of sharing truth with charity.

You can leave your feedback wherever you purchased the book or on your preferred platform. Every kind word, thoughtful insight, or shared experience means the world to me—and helps others searching for the fullness of faith find their way home too.

With gratitude and in Christ,

Kristie

"To be deep in history is to cease to be Protestant."

—*An Essay on the Development of Christian Doctrine*, Venerable John Henry Newman

(Anglican priest turned Catholic cardinal)

Special Thanks

Pope Francis (Jorge Mario Bergoglio)
December 17, 1936–April 21, 2025

To Pope Francis, my first Holy Father.

Thank you for leading the Church with humility, courage, and a heart wide open to the mercy of God. Your witness to Christ's love has inspired me deeply, and I am forever grateful to have entered the Catholic Church under your pontificate.

May your legacy of compassion and truth continue to echo in the hearts of all who seek the face of Christ.

About the Author

Pictured L-R: Deacon Tom Cabeen, Kristie, her husband Eric,
Fr. Robert Healey, Associate Pastor of St. Francis Xavier Catholic Church,
Stillwater, OK

Kristie is a recovering Protestant with a well-worn map of every denominational detour imaginable—including a pitstop in the occult (10/10, do not recommend). After years of spiritual wandering and whiplash—thanks to God's mercy and an army of praying saints and family members, she and her husband finally came home to the Catholic Church. Her confirmation saint is St. Teresa of Ávila: mystic, reformer, Doctor of the Church, and spiritual spitfire. Seemed fitting.

Kristie lives in Oklahoma, wrangling a lively crew of three grown (and equally stubborn) sons, two teenage granddaughters, and three dogs who think they own the place. Caffeinated and consecrated, she's spent the last decade co-running Archangel Ink, a self-publishing firm she and her friend Rob Archangel built to help authors turn their ideas into polished, purposeful books, and leave a written legacy they can be proud of. Something she hopes to do as well.

Inspirational Works Cited & References

Sacred Scripture

All Scripture references are taken from the Holy Bible. Unless otherwise noted, quotations are from the Revised Standard Version–Catholic Edition (RSV-CE).

Church Councils and Official Church Documents

- Catechism of the Catholic Church, 2nd Edition. Libreria Editrice Vaticana, 1997.

- The Documents of Vatican II. Walter M. Abbott, ed. America Press, 1966.

- Council of Nicaea I (325 AD) and Council of Constantinople I (381 AD).

- Council of Trent (1545–1563). Decrees and Canons.

- Code of Canon Law. Vatican.va

Church Fathers and Early Christian Writings

- St. Ignatius of Antioch. *Letters*, c. 107 AD.

- St. Irenaeus of Lyons. *Against Heresies*, c. 180 AD.

- St. Justin Martyr. *First Apology*, c. 155 AD.

- St. Cyril of Jerusalem. *Catechetical Lectures*, c. 350 AD.

- Tertullian. *On the Flesh of Christ*, c. 200 AD.

- The *Didache* (Teaching of the Twelve Apostles), c. 70–90 AD.

Biblical & Historical Scholarship

- Hahn, Scott. *The Fourth Cup: Unveiling the Mystery of the Last Supper and the Cross*. Image Books, 2018.

- Hahn, Scott. *Rome Sweet Home: Our Journey to Catholicism*. Ignatius Press, 1993.

- Kreeft, Peter. *Catholic Christianity: A Complete Catechism of Catholic Beliefs*. Ignatius Press, 2001.

- Newman, John Henry. *An Essay on the Development of Christian Doctrine*. 1845.

- Ratzinger, Joseph (Pope Benedict XVI). *Jesus of Nazareth* series.

Eucharistic Miracles and the Shroud of Turin

- Gruber, Michael. *The Eucharistic Miracles of the World*. Real Presence Eucharistic Education and Adoration Association, 2009.

- Zugibe, Frederick. *The Crucifixion of Jesus: A Forensic Inquiry*. M. Evans & Company, 2005.

- National Catholic Register. Articles on Eucharistic Miracles and the Shroud of Turin. (see Real Presence Eucharistic Education and Adoration Association)

- Vatican Research on the Shroud of Turin (STURP reports).

Lanciano, Italy (8th Century) Scientific Study (1970s):

Conducted by Dr. Odoardo Linoli, a professor of anatomy and pathological histology, with assistance from Dr. Ruggero Bertelli, a professor of human anatomy at the University of Siena.

Source & Report:

1. Linoli, O. (1971). Ricerche istologiche, immunologiche e biochi-
miche su campioni prelevati dal miracolo eucaristico di Lanciano.
[Histological, immunological, and biochemical research on samples
taken from the Eucharistic Miracle of Lanciano]

2. English summary by the Real Presence Eucharistic Education and
Adoration Association:
https://therealpresence.org/eucharst/mir/lanciano.html

3. Additional commentary and analysis (with citations):
https://www.miracolieucaristici.org/en/Lanciano/

Buenos Aires, Argentina (1996) Scientific Studies (2000s–2005):

Samples examined by Dr. Ricardo Castañón Gómez (formerly an atheist
neuropsychologist turned Catholic). Further analysis by cardiologist
Dr. Frederick Zugibe, then a forensic pathology expert in New York.

Sources:

1. Documentary summary by Dr. Castañón Gómez (with English
subtitles): https://www.youtube.com/watch?v=qbg_dhI4XCs

2. Real Presence Association summary:
https://therealpresence.org/eucharst/mir/english_pdf/BuenosAires3.pdf

3. Secondary medical commentary referencing Zugibe's analysis:
https://aleteia.org/2015/10/12/miracle-in-argentina-scientific-ana
lysis-of-a-consecrated-host/

Sokolka, Poland (2008) Scientific Analysis (2009–2010):

Conducted at the Medical University of Białystok. Two pathologists,
Dr. Maria Sobaniec-Łotowska and Dr. Stanisław Sulkowski, confirmed
presence of myocardial tissue fused with the bread in a way that ruled
out fabrication.

Sources:

1. Official report from Polish diocese:
   https://sokolka.archibial.pl/miracle

2. Real Presence Association summary:
   https://therealpresence.org/eucharst/mir/english_pdf/Sokolka.pdf

3. English article overviewing the findings:
   https://aleteia.org/2015/10/12/miracle-in-poland-consecrated-ho
   st-becomes-heart-tissue/

Statistical & Abuse Reports

- John Jay College of Criminal Justice. *The Nature and Scope of Sexual Abuse of Minors by Catholic Priests and Deacons in the United States, 1950–2002,* 2004.

- U.S. Department of Education. *Educator Sexual Misconduct: A Synthesis of Existing Literature,* Charol Shakeshaft, 2004.

- Center for Applied Research in the Apostolate. Reports on Church demographics and abuse prevention.

Anti-Catholicism in America:

- See Mark A. Noll, *The Old Religion in a New World: The History of North American Christianity* (2001), which explores how American Protestantism and suspicion of hierarchy shaped religious culture. Also consider the legacy of the "Know-Nothing Party" (1850s), an anti-Catholic political movement based on fears of Catholic loyalty to the Pope over American democracy.

- Catholic teaching on salvation emphasizes salvation by grace through faith, working in love (Galatians 5:6; James 2:24), and condemns Pelagianism (the heresy of salvation by human effort alone).

- See George Weigel, *The Irony of Modern Catholic History* (2019), which details how modern secular movements often targeted the Church as an obstacle to progress. Media bias against Catholic moral teaching has also been documented across decades, particularly regarding issues like abortion, marriage, and religious freedom.

Resources for Further Study

Here's a curated list of **book recommendations for deeper research** on Catholic theology, Church history, the early Church, Marian doctrines, the Eucharist, and conversion stories—especially great for continuing your journey or helping others explore **the truth** of Catholicism.

Conversion Stories & Apologetics

- *Rome Sweet Home*-Scott & Kimberly Hahn

- *Crossing the Tiber*-Steve Ray

- *Surprised by Truth* (Volumes 1-3)-ed. Patrick Madrid

- *Evangelical Is Not Enough*-Thomas Howard

- *Why We're Catholic*-Trent Horn

- *The Case for Catholicism*-Trent Horn

- *Answering the Protestant Challenge*-Karlo Broussard

Early Church & Church History

- *Four Witnesses: The Early Church in Her Own Words*-Rod Bennett

- *The Fathers Know Best*-Jimmy Akin

- *The Mass of the Early Christians*-Mike Aquilina

- *Pope Peter: Defending the Church's Most Distinctive Doctrine in a Time of Crisis*-Joe Heschmeyer

- *The Early Church Was the Catholic Church*-Joe Heschmeyer

- *Jesus and the Jewish Roots of the Papacy*-Brant Pitre

- *Answering Orthodoxy: A Catholic Response to Attacks from the East*–Michael Lofton

- *The Papacy: Revisiting the Debate Between Catholics and Orthodox*–Erick Ybarra

Theology & Scripture

- *Catholic Christianity*–Peter Kreeft

- *Behold Your Mother*–Tim Staples

- *Hail, Holy Queen*–Scott Hahn

- *Salvation: What Every Catholic Should Know*–Michael Barber

- *A Biblical Walk Through the Mass*–Edward Sri

- *Jesus and the Jewish Roots of the Eucharist*–Brant Pitre

- *Jesus and the Jewish Roots of Mary*–Brant Pitre

- *Jesus and the Jewish Roots of the Papacy*–Brant Pitre

- *A Catholic Introduction to the Bible: Old Testament*–John Bergsma & Brant Pitre

- *Bible Basics for Catholics*–John Bergsma

- *Jesus and the Dead Sea Scrolls: Revealing the Jewish Roots of Christianity*–John Bergsma

- *The Eucharist Is Really Jesus: How Christ's Body and Blood Are the Key to Everything We Believe*–Joe Heschmeyer

Recommended YouTube Channels for Catholic Apologetics:

- **The No-Nonsense Catholic–Matthew Arnold**
  🔗 youtube.com/@vmpradio
  Straightforward, orthodox Catholic teaching delivered in an easy-to-understand style.

- **The Counsel of Trent–Trent Horn**
  🔗 youtube.com/@TheCounselofTrent
  A Catholic Answers apologist known for respectful debates and thoughtful answers to objections against Catholicism.

- **Reason & Theology–Michael Lofton**
  🔗 youtube.com/@ReasonandTheology
  A go-to source for in-depth interviews and theological dialogue with experts across Catholicism, Orthodoxy, and Protestantism.

- **Catholic Ecclesiastica**
  🔗 youtube.com/@CatholicEcclesiastica
  Beautifully produced videos explaining Catholic theology, liturgy, and Church history using a scholarly and accessible approach.

- **Erick Ybarra**
  🔗 youtube.com/@ErickYbarra
  Focused on Catholic-Orthodox dialogue, magisterial authority, and patristics. Rich in citations and deeply researched theology.

- **Suan Sonna–Intellectual Catholic**
  🔗 youtube.com/@IntellectualCatholic
  A philosophy and theology channel offering deep dives into Thomism, biblical evidence for Catholicism, and interviews with Catholic thinkers.

- **Jimmy Akin–Jimmy Akin's Mysterious World**
  🔗 youtube.com/@JimmyAkin
  Explores Catholic theology, history, Scripture, and fascinating mysteries from a faithful and reasoned Catholic perspective.

- **Joe Heschmeyer–Shameless Popery**
  🔗 youtube.com/@ShamelessPopery
  A former lawyer turned priest and Catholic apologist offering accessible and thoughtful defenses of Catholic doctrine.

- **Dr. Alan Harrelson – The Pipe Cottage**
  🔗 youtube.com/@ThePipeCottage
  A Southern historian and convert to Catholicism who blends pipe-smoking charm with intellectual commentary on history, tradition, and the Catholic faith.

www.ingramcontent.com/pod-product-compliance
Lightning Source LLC
LaVergne TN
LVHW041316080426
835513LV00008B/478